Always shine &
Journey on

♡

Jess

:)

Almost Zima +

Jamira or

♡

:)

The
journey
behind
my shine

The
journey
behind
my shine

A true story

Jessica Zacharias

To order additional copies of this book, contact:
Xlibris
1-888-795-4274
www.Xlibris.com
Orders@Xlibris.com
732422

CONTENTS

I dedicate this to my ego for allowing my soul to lead
this journey in order for it to shine its true light.

Preface

"You are going to be a writer," she said.

Excuse me? What? I don't think so, missy. There is no way that is going to happen. You must be crazy, I thought to myself.

"Keep journaling. Write everything down. You are going to be a writer," she insisted.

Summer of 2014 is when I received that message. Fast-forward to now, and look! She was right. See here is the thing: the beautiful soul who shared that message with me is a soul that is in a different realm of the universe. Secretly, I knew she was right. But holy cow was I unaware on what I was getting myself into.

Keep in mind this is my first book. I am blunt, which you will find. People my age are in nine-to-five jobs, moving to different states, or planning to continue with their education, which God bless them- that is great!

You will find my journey is one that tends to swerve off the "ideal" path. Always has and always will. For the past year, Barnes & Noble, Starbucks, and various tea places have served as my nine-to-five job.

This was my way of healing and to start living my journey rather than running away from it. I allowed myself to rewrite my story and to also share it.

Yeah, I know you may be thinking what "wisdom" does this chick have? However, I encourage you to grab some tea, put some soothing music on, and journey on with me.

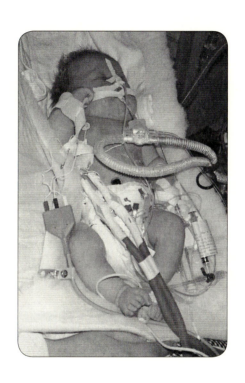

An Uncertain World

I do not remember much about the day—I mean, how could I? I just took my first look of this unknown place. Everything happened so fast. I did not get the chance to be held by my parents or relatives, so I was alone but curious of this place. I was just a couple of hours old when I got to experience my first ride in an ambulance. Lights were flashing and sirens were blasting as I was experiencing the rush of urgency this world has. Tubes of all sizes were put into my body, and hands were touching me without my permission, which I thought was normal. April 28, 1993, is when my journey on this world began. It serves as a day that traumatized my family. Me, on the other hand, I knew it was just the beginning of my discovery of this uncertain world.

I was born with a birth defect called TEF, tracheoesophageal fistula. To save you from attending a science class, I will put it in simpler terms. As humans, we have an esophagus and a trachea. They work together to push our food down into our stomachs. When all goes well, no choking or it-went-down-the-wrong-pipe moments happen. Well, mine were not connected, so I was a blue baby, which meant I was not breathing. Literally the color of the ocean or sky. Just five seconds into my new journey on this world, I was not normal. When you Google TEF, it literally states it is a congenital abnormality. As you can see, I was off to a great start, standing out in this unknown world. No wonder the word "normal" always makes me flinch.

I needed extra attention and help (no surprise there), and I was rushed to Children's Hospital of Michigan down in Detroit. My body was as fragile as fine china. Honestly, my body was probably saying, "Screw this place." Every moment counted. My mother was experiencing a labor nightmare and was hollering as to why she could not hold her newborn baby girl, let alone even see me. My father had to make a decision to either stay with my mom in the hospital or follow their first child down to Detroit. The day that is all worked up by hosting parties and making the house into a family home became nothing but red-black fear.

I was just a day old when I was operated on. The goal was to try to connect my esophagus and trachea, so they had to cut me open from my back, near my shoulder blade, across my underarm, and under my breast. They were doing anything they could to save my life and not thinking about the damage the scars would create later on.

I learned from day one how scary and uncertain this world can be. By this point, the only eye contact I received was from people with blue or white masks on covering their mouths and blue nets around their head. The only human touch I received was nothing but latex gloves. I lay alone in an incubator for six days before seeing my mother. The first time my dad held me, I was taped to a board. A tube was down my nose to help me breathe, and another tube came out of my sides to drain the fluids. My incubator was in the NICU, which served as my home for over a month before I got to go to my new home. My parents made my incubator as homey as they could. My dad put a pink stuffed puppy in my incubator, which, to this day, has never left my side. Seriously, I am twenty-two years old, and I still sleep with my friend named Lucky. I even bring him with me when I travel. It serves as my reminder of where I started from and how blessed I am to experience whatever it is in that moment.

Family came to visit, but doctors really did not know how long I would have on this earth. They estimated three years. Why? Because my birth defect started to create problems within my body, and I would stop breathing at any given moment. Literally just living life and then boom—I go down. Babysitters refused to watch me because I was consistent on living inconsistently. I frightened them with the life aspect on how fragile this life really is. Plus, the amount of steroids and medicine they were giving my poor little body would most likely cause problems down the road, but they weren't focused on keeping me alive forever. They, which they should, just focused on one day at a time.

Because of my birth defect, I had to be fed through a feeding tube. When I was a baby, I was fed through the tubes up my nose; but when my body got a little bit bigger, I actually had a tube in my stomach. Fast-forward to now, no wonder I love chipotle so much. The tube did do its job, but once a month, it had to be replaced—meaning, my parents would sneak into my room at night and quickly pull it out of my stomach and place a new one in. Imagine the horror and pain I felt having a tube in my stomach and having it get ripped out of me. Talk about trust issues and being sensitive to who I allowed to touch my body.

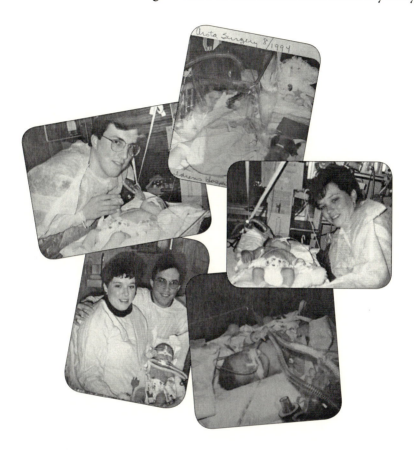

My body had no control over the pathway food traveled down to get to my stomach. My doctors wrapped half of my stomach around the bottom of my esophagus to allow the food to go down—meaning, I cannot physically vomit. No, don't wish you had this even though it sounds like a cool thing to have. Here is the issue: My body experiences the same symptoms yours has when you experience the moment when you get sick. I experience the hot flashes, dizziness, and overall weakness. But my body is confused and tries its hardest to come up a path it is meant to come up. So when I need to get sick, I become a patient in the hospital with a tube up her nose down to my stomach sucking out the vomit. I dry heave, and it sounds like I am dying. Literally. I also pass gas because my body is trying to release all the toxins but does not know how.

Also, whenever I sneeze or cough, no one knows how to respond because they both sound the same. But when I sneeze, I sneeze at least four times in a row.

After many surgeries, procedures, and adventures to the hospital, I made it past my three-year life expectancy! Woohoo! Plus, I got a little baby brother, literally my partner in crime in all my imagination games, concerts, or activities I would come up with in our household.

I started kindergarten and enjoyed going to school and hanging out with friends. My doctors cleared me for sports and physical activities, which made me so happy. I actually felt like I fit in for once in my life!

Even though I went through a lot in my early childhood, I made sure I treated every day like it was a gift and treated everyone with kindness because you really never know what kind of day they are having. Secretly, I invited my whole class to my birthday party without asking my mom if that was okay. She just thought the girls were coming—surprise! Everyone came.

My kindergarten class was one of a kind. To this day, I still keep in contact with a couple of my best friends I met in that class. It was a journey growing up with them, but boy, was it fun. I truly believe everyone that comes into your journey teaches you a lesson, no matter if it is good, bad, or ugly. You learn something from them, and that alone is essential for growth.

For instance, one day back in first grade, my friend came over, and we wanted to fly. We found some pixie dust and dumped all the bottles on each other's head and ran from one end of the hallway all the way down into my bedroom and flew onto my bed. We did that for at least two hours. When her mom picked her up, she was confused as to why she had so much glitter in her hair.

"We believe we can fly," we said together and laughed.

It was cute at first, but weeks later, glitter was still shining in our hair. To this day, we are each other's encouragers, opening each other's wings to fly.

Growing up means many things, but it also means your body changes. The body is a magnificent masterpiece and always inspires me. One thing I must point out—if you haven't noticed already—is that, yes, my insides and the connection between my head and body is not so normal. However, the outside of my body looks as healthy as healthy can be. I feel as if I serve as the living proof of the saying "Don't judge a book by its cover." My mom told me stories about how she would take me to all sorts of therapy since I needed it and how many rude stares she would get. People would ask her why she was bringing me to such therapy session and to make a point she would pick me up and show them my feeding tube and all my scars. The whole feeding tube chapter lasted up until second grade.

I am a person who normally does not wear anything form-fitting because I don't like to bring extra unnecessary attention to my scars. Here is the back story.

Imagine innocent little Jessica playing outside underneath a tree. I love everything about trees, so no surprise I was exploring the land around one. Anyway, one of my classmates became curious as to why there was a bump on my stomach. That day, I wore a form-fitting shirt, so the tube was more obvious than other days. My classmate pulled on the tube, which ended up coming out. Yeah, typical Jessica moment. My dad had to come to the school because I was so terrified and very emotional. Once he picked me up, he took me to the hospital where my doctor decided my esophagus and trachea were strong enough to not use the tube anymore. Blessing in disguise, I would say.

An appointment was made, and it was time to take the tube out and really learn how to eat and swallow. No eating after 6:00 p.m., no eating popcorn, only eat soft foods, elevate your bed, drink a least one cup of water after every meal, take your breathing treatment, eat slowly, my doctors would say to make sure my food would stay in my stomach. That was easy when I was little, but growing up in this uncertain world, that became a challenge I hardly expected.

Since the skin is the largest organ on the body, it can heal itself if you allow time to do its work. My tube was in my stomach for around six years, so my skin around the tube was used to not being connected. I lay on the patient table, staring up at the yellow light, feeling my doctor lift my shirt, place one hand on my tube, and rested his arm on my hips so I would not flail and resist the procedure. Before I knew it, I was screaming and hollering because the pain of the tube being pulled out of my stomach was taking over. He then stitched me up, which I made it difficult for him to do. I mean, can you blame me? I was a young kid getting a feeding tube pulled out of me! Of course, I am going to make a scene.

I somehow, someway, found the positive in every situation, no matter how challenging it was. Later, I realized it was not me that was doing that. Something much greater than me was coming through.

After my sob fest, my mom and I stopped by my grandparents' house to give them an update. Plus, I thought it was kind of cool to show people my stitches. I am no stranger to stitches, so I know how it feels when the body and the skin start to heal. But this time, I felt different. A huge bandage was wrapped around my stomach, and I was told not to touch it or itch it or play with it. Talk about learning how to be responsible at a young age.

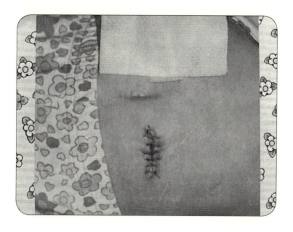

My grandparents and my mom were in the kitchen, and I was sitting in my grandma's big girl chair occupying myself. I kept thinking about how cold my wound felt and how it has never felt like that before. Disobeying my doctor's orders and listening to what my body was telling me, I lifted my shirt, peeled off my bandage, took a quick glance at my stitches, and realized my stitches were coming undone. I had a hole the size of a quarter on my stomach. At the age of seven, I saw the inside of my stomach. I remember my mom running over to see why I lifted my shirt, and before I could comprehend it, she was driving on the highway with me screaming in the backseat because the hole did not stop expanding. You know, it is kind of sad when you enter the hospital and every worker knows you and your family. My mom must have called my doctor on the way there because as soon as we pulled up into the half-circle drive with the small rainbow in the corner of the building, I, Jessica Helene Zacharias, was the center of attention once again.

They got it under control, but my skin was stubborn and would not connect. I literally had to go on with my life with a hole in my stomach. Obviously, they had gauze strips from side to side to pull it together, but they couldn't put me under, so the pressure and pain my body felt as my doctor's hands were doing everything they could to squeeze my stomach back to one piece was a feeling I hope no one has to fight through.

Just a couple of days after that, we were supposed to leave for Florida to go to Sea World and Disney World. My parents got an awesome room next to all the pools and water slides. I was so excited to go! But then my parents had to break the news to me that I could not get my stomach wet.

I vividly remember having to sit on the concrete and dip my little toes in the water because my stomach was not healed yet. I was so angry and upset. I was confused as to why I had to go through this. Watching everyone else have fun and do what he or she wanted really became a challenge for me. A challenge that I still face today. My brother and my dad tried not to rub it in, and they went to other pools to swim, but that was when I first really was conscious enough to understand what was really going on.

The scar healed and became a warrior mark. It is in a shape of a sun with a straight line through it. That's the thing about my health journey—when you look at me, I look like an everyday normal human being, but behind the clothes, I have nine large scars. Now I am not complaining, I have been blessed with an eventful journey, but I will say it does have its positives and negatives, especially trying to make it alive in this world.

Around this time, my doctors became aware of how I was still aspirating into my lungs even though my stomach was wrapped. Similar terms, whenever I burp or cough, I am aspirating into my lungs. After many scopes and breathing tests, my body was diagnosed with restrictive lung disease. No, it is not asthma, but it is similar. My lung capacity is around 67 percent when majority of you have at least 90 percent. So when you ask me to run a mile or workout for a long period, you will most likely get a sassy face from me.

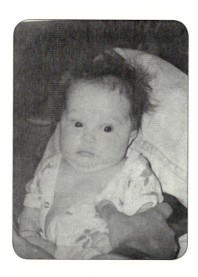

Not to be rude, but to never judge a book by its cover. This became challenging in gym class and even being active in general. I always did my best to avoid a Jessica moment in front of my classmates or teammates. I did not really accept myself just yet. I mean, to be honest, I thought everyone went to the doctor as much as I did. I was still learning about this uncertain world. I just kept learning more and more each day.

After my lung diagnosis, traveling to other states, such as Ohio, was needed. My doctors wanted to make sure I was getting the best of the best, so I just left the business stuff up to my parents, and I went with it, some days not willingly, but in order to survive, I had to. My parents were tough and turned a trip to the doctors into a vacation—meaning, let's say I had a surgery planned on Wednesday. The weekend before, we would go to an amusement park, museum, or beach. Mom and Dad, high five for this parenting technique, because looking back on it now, that was an essential part of my mental strength and the journey it took.

As I got older, I became vocal about my beliefs on what was going on with my body. I became protective of it and always tried to listen to it. It was in middle school after I broke my arm twice, sprained my wrist, and broke my pinkie finger that I was diagnosed with osteopenia and vitamin D deficiency. My bones are as strong as old grandma bones, and without having any vitamin D, the calcium I did have was not absorbing properly.

"You might as well move to Florida and live with cows for the rest of you life," Dr. Bones joked. Yes, his name is really Dr. Bones.

It would take years to build strong healthy bones. Since I was tube fed the thought of milk makes me want to gag. My calcium numbers were not even on the chart—that is how weak my bones were. Why? Most likely due to the steroids I was put on as a little kid. I thought after my journey of breaking and spraining my arms, my bone health would get better; instead, it did the opposite. I never knew what a shin splint was until I had them consistently my junior and senior year of high school. I became a pro at showering with a cast on and even swimming in the ocean with a garbage bag wrapped around an area on my body.

Of course, when I broke my left arm for the second time, my journey decided to sprain my right arm too. Talk about Jessica the robot. Try balancing your schoolbooks through the hallways. I never understood why calcium was so important to your health until I was forced to. That is the thing about my health journey. I did not choose any of my illnesses or diseases—they just came to me. Obviously, I know there is a reason behind all of it, but gosh darn it, and I tried so hard to not let it define who I was; but once high school came around, I became a stranger to myself.

It was a summer day when all my neighbors and I were swimming and playing outside in my backyard when I got the news. I recently had to get my blood drawn because there was news that a blood disorder runs in the family, and we all needed to get checked. Would you look at that, I can add another illness to my list. It is called Factor Five, which means after the fifth cell in my blood, if I don't move for a certain amount of time, my blood will clot, which would then go travel through my bloodstream and cause all sorts of problems that could be deadly. At the time, I did not have to worry, but the disorder is what was common in females who would die during labor. A positive is that I found out early. However, it would cause all sorts of female issues down the road. When I started to have my female cycle, I became very physically and emotionally exhausted. My mother had me tested because I was in a funk for so long, and turns out, I am anemic too—which would make sense. Iron is in the blood, which you lose a lot of during the cycle, so at least I had an answer on why I felt so tired and weak. But let me tell you, going to a female doctor when you are that young and sitting with a bunch of pregnant people wasn't awkward at all.

My birth defect also affected my teeth and my speech. Growing up, my mom took me to speech class, and to this day, if you listen really closely, I still cannot pronounce some words, like jewelry or sausage. Once all my baby teeth were out, my big girl teeth started to come in. Well, let me rephrase, they were coming in whatever way they wanted—meaning, some of my teeth were growing up toward my nose. When my orthodontist saw my X-rays, he could not believe what he saw.

He is one of a kind, and my mom actually had him as an orthodontist. He cares so much for his patients, but he is not afraid to call you out on not wearing your rubber bands or brushing your teeth. Instead of saying, "Okay, now open up," he says, "Okay, open your face." He listens to politics and news every morning, drinks coffee out of the same cup, and works out at the same gym and time every single day. He set up an appointment for me to see a surgeon and have some of my teeth exposed, so then he could place brackets on my teeth to align them.

Cue looking like a chipmunk for months. The surgery was planned, and I forgot how during a mouth or tooth surgery, they just numb your mouth so your eyes and ears are still open. Hearing the drills and seeing blood flying out of my mouth was enough for me to lose it. Once again, the deep anger I had toward my body and this universe became present again.

Once the surgery was done, I had to go to my orthodontist the next day. Time was sensitive, and I got braces. My mouth was still very sore from the surgery, so I had to wear gum gauze for a couple of weeks. It literally looked like a piece of gum was stuck in my braces. Weeks go by of feeling like crap because everyone is asking why I have gum stuck in my braces. But it was time for it to come off and to see how my exposed tooth looked. My orthodontist pulled off the gauze, and I will never forget the shock in his face. I was lying on my back in the orthodontist chair just confused as to why his face was in horror.

"Shoot. You have got to be kidding. This has never happened before," he said.

Talk about having an emotional breakdown inside. I am assuming I gave him my bitch face because I was in need of an answer.

"Your teeth are not in the right order," he said quietly.

"What does that mean?" I asked.

"It means there are two teeth that switched spots," he explained.

"So my teeth aren't normal?" I asked.

"That is correct. But don't worry—they are special. I can shape them to look the way they are supposed to, if you want," he comforted me.

I don't even know if I responded. I just lay back, closed my eyes to fight the tears, and let him figure out what the next step was.

My braces were a part of my smile for four years. Talk about a long process, especially when you are in high school. Ironically, enough years pass, and I become one of his assistants! One of the best jobs I ever had.

There have been many challenges but also many steps forward in my health journey. One thing that won't change is the fact that no matter where I go for medical treatment, I will always be the patient that stirs up conversations and interest. Whenever I would walk into my physical therapy place, I would hear them say, "Why hello! Our mess is here." Of course, I love them all, and I have had to continuously go back there many times, but moral of the story is you get used to it after a while. I had two choices whenever a situation would present itself. Either let it define me or I define it. I strive to define it every single time.

My body and my journey is one of a kind. My body questions the idea of medicine, and my journey is nowhere to be found in the books professionals studied for years. Kind of feel bad for them every time I see a new doctor. They have the attitude of "She looks healthy, so I am just going to listen on what hurts and tell her what to do," and then they open up my chart, and it is as if they were treating a celebrity. Their persona changes.

I know it is a lot to remember, so I'll break it down for you. Here is a list of what we have covered so far:

TEF
Cannot vomit/stomach tied
Restrictive lung disease—food aspirates into my lungs
Feeding tube
Osteopenia/vitamin D deficiency
Factor Five
Anemic

At this point, I have had at least over thirty surgeries and medical procedures done!

And this is just the beginning . . . Hold on tight, friends!

Soul Movement

It wasn't until my sophomore year of high school when I really learned the importance of dance and movement and how much weight it held for my overall wellness. Yes, obviously, I knew exercise was good for the body, and it kept me active, but I was not aware of the healing energy it provided. I would be lost without dance. Doctors say that is what kept me going. Looking back on it, dance has been my best friend and has never left me. The times when I hated my body and my self-confidence was low, dance and movement brought love to it. When I felt joyful and happy, dance lets me express it. Being able to express emotions through movement is something I urge everyone to try at least once in their life.

Fall was in the air, and it was time to learn the choreography for my new solo. This year my teacher decided to spice it up and change the genre I would be performing. Usually, I would perform jazz or sassy musical theater, but she was a teacher that pushed me. She challenged me in ways I will always be grateful for. When she told me what I would be dancing for, I froze.

"You are going to perform your story by moving and performing a lyrical contemporary piece." She said like it was nothing challenging at all. I looked like a deer in headlights because I never really opened up about my health and my journey in this way before. Yes, people know a little bit, but they just know the positive I-made-it story. Not the dark days where fighting for my life took place. They aren't aware of my silent tears I cry from time to time because I stood as a girl who was afraid to show any type of weakness. I finally got the confidence to ask her to repeat her statement to make sure I understood her properly, but before I could finish my question, she interrupted and said, "You are going to pretend like there is a wall dividing the stage. One side is the dark side, and the other is the positive side. Your starting position will be on the ground, curled up in a ball against the wall on the dark side."

She was not kidding. She was the first person throughout my journey that opened up a door to a sense of discovery and self-fulfillment. The dance was not physically tiring, but the emotional piece behind it made it difficult to accomplish. Whenever I felt good about it, she insisted that I would do it again and push harder. There was a time when I somehow banged my head on the ground during the piece, but she still motivated me to keep going.

Now I am a pretty private person when it comes to personal stuff because what I have learned and gone through at my age has been an invitation to chill on my own island with my lessons and beliefs. I am the enlightener, the wise one or the angel of the group. I would guide others and be fulfilled by it. But this was the first time when someone was guiding me. I did not want to disappoint her or myself.

It was a beautiful day outside, and she scheduled an extra practice because she believed I needed to focus on expressing more emotion. Let me tell you, there was no emotion to be found that day. I was tired, stressed from dealing with high school stuff. She and I were the only two in the studio for over a long period. She told me that she would keep me there until the next morning if I didn't express my true emotions. I glanced up and saw my dad walk into the studio. God bless him. Growing up, he tried so hard to be there for my family, but work always got in the way. So it put a little damper on our relationship, but when he walked in to watch me practice, my emotions danced their way out of my body like they were free at last. My soul was dancing and guiding me through the piece.

After I was done with the piece, I ran to the bathroom and cried. I have never felt so much emotion in my life and especially showing that much emotion in front of people. I was vulnerable and did not have any care in the world on what the world may think of my emotions. I sat in the studio bathroom for about five minutes until I got my emotions under control. As I opened the door, my dad was there with his arms wide open. My teacher was sobbing because she knew I did it. After that practice, I was ready to perform it at competition. I was a warrior who found the strength to share my story with others.

Now am I a good dancer? Sure, if you say so. But since that moment when I move and dance, it is my soul that is doing the job. Honor my soul rather than me personally about my dancing talent.

Competitions were weekends I felt like I was in heaven. Well, besides the early mornings, putting on fake eyelashes, or having your costume rack breaking on the way into the school, leaving your costumes all over the parking lot, it was a weekend where the energy was high and memories were made. On top of performing, our families would barbeque, get hotel rooms, and we would just live life to the fullest. One of my favorite aspects about competitions was witnessing another dances and viewing their beauty.

Solos usually would be on Friday nights, and then the rest of my dances would be Saturday and Sunday. I enjoyed having my solo first because it set a foundation for the rest of the week. Plus, I would be the first to feel the stage, get to make my mark on it, and to feel comfortable performing on it.

My solo was called "My Truth," and the song was a piano piece by Yann Tiersen. My teacher's reasoning behind picking an instrumental piece was to allow my body and movements to tell my story.

The weekend of the first competition arrived. Nerves, as well as excitement, were present all week at the studio. The time had finally arrived for me to perform my solo, with my costume, hair, and makeup. It was a divine evening, I would say. My teacher came to my house, and my parents, myself, and my teacher all drove together to the competition. They were all excited to watch me up on that stage and encouraged me to do my best. We arrived to the competition, and my parents ventured their way to the auditorium as my teacher guided me to a hallway to practice. I warmed up my body and got in the zone. I checked myself in backstage; my teacher gave me a huge hug and then went into the auditorium to watch. So this was it, my time to shine.

As I stood in the wings backstage, my hands started to tingle, and my heart started beating out of my chest. I knew it was just my nerves getting to me, so I closed my eyes, took some deep breaths, and started doing my happy dance, which includes jumping like a monkey and flailing my arms around. The dancer before me was coming to the end of her dance, so I knew there was no turning back.

"Please welcome to the stage, Jessica Zacharias, performing 'My Truth,' from Gotta Dance Studios."

I heard my parents and my teacher clapping and cheering me on as the stage lights shone on me. I walked on that stage with my chin held high and knew what my assignment was.

As I got into position, I whispered to myself, "Let's do this." My music started playing, and I allowed my soul to dance. It was if I were on top of the world performing this beautiful meaningful piece. I became vulnerable and ended my solo by standing in the front of the stage with my arms wide open, accepting what is. People I didn't even know were coming up to me after and saying how much they enjoyed my dance. Honored, of course, but I get awkward with attention. It was awards time, and I always enjoyed cheering for the other competitors. The way this competition is set up for overall highest scores is that they play your music and make a huge deal out of your accomplishment. After announcing the nine highest scores, it was time to announce the winning routine. Not going to lie, I was ready to leave the stage and get some food, but I thought it would be the bigger person of me to stay onstage and congratulate the first place winner. I am sitting dreaming about food and most likely my bed when the winning music starts to play. I think to myself, "Hey, this sounds familiar," but then I go back to thinking about food. It was when one of my studio friends interrupted my daydream by grabbing my shoulders and said, "Jess, you won!"

I was ecstatic. I could not believe it. I could hear my parents and teacher cheering, as well as everyone else in the audience. All eyes were on me, and boy was in a memorable moment. I received some cash, a big trophy, and the title for the highest-scoring solo of the night. Now, yes, the cash and the trophy were nice, but they didn't mean as much to me as you may think. To me, those materialistic objects last a couple of years or so. For me to take that step to express my scars and dark days without fear was enough for me. I already knew I achieved my assignment. Since that moment, my friendship with dance became my number one priority.

The studio I grew up in will always be my second home. My teachers challenged me, motivated me, and allowed me to shine. My classmates are my tribe. Each one of them taught me a lesson. We would know everything about one another: shoe size, hair color, school they went to, family members, dislikes and likes, boyfriends and friend drama. They were the special souls who knew of my journey and who still danced with me when I was nothing but a broken shattered mess trying to pick up the pieces.

For my last couple of years at the studio, my group, as a whole, grew in more ways than one. We got the honor to perform a piece in honor of a girl who was diagnosed with a brain tumor. The opportunity allowed me to realize how dance not only could heal you but it can heal others too. It moves people in ways verbal communication cannot. We became a living proof of how essential soul movement is to this world and how it is our mission to share that life lesson with others. For me, it was my master key to being able to share my scars in more ways than one on a soul level. And to be able to teach and share my passion with my students brings my scars even more light. Thank you, my Gotta Dance family, for providing a space for me to move through my darkness and to allow me to shine in more ways than one.

The Color Yellow

I was a junior in high school when my family and I went on a cruise for my spring break. It was our first time as a family going on a cruise for a week, so needless to say, it was going to be an adventure.

Each day we had a different agenda, which made the week fly by. The third day, all the families signed up to swim with stingrays. Not going to lie, I was nervous. Nerves danced through my body as the thought of animals swimming around me crossed my mind.

As we were getting ready for the day, I had this strange outside force feeling. I felt as if I was being protected, but I did not know why. For the next couple of hours, I was in a slow-motion movie. I was calm and gentle. My eyes kept wandering off to search for the cause of this unique energy. I tried to be discreet about it, so I just kept to myself, but the feeling kept getting stronger and stronger—almost like the universe was preparing me for something.

We were at the table eating breakfast when my mom begged me to take my pills.

"Please just take your pills. We are going to be in the sun all day long," she said.

She did have a point, I thought to myself, so unwillingly, I swallowed all my pills with a fake smile on my face as the pills slowly made their way down my broken esophagus. As we were venturing to the boat that was going to take us to shore, I felt lightheaded. I kept quiet because I did not want attention and just hoped my body was having a quick short and sweet moment.

At a stop, one of our moms took this picture. You can see my sunglasses are on and that smile is definitely forced.

After riding a boat and an hour bus ride, we finally made it to our destination boat with the stingrays. The boat was inviting and had two levels full of fun. My friends and I thought, why not go on the top and embrace the sun?

This is where it gets exciting. In order to get to the top, you must climb a ladder. Simple right? Yeah, I thought the same thing.

As I was climbing, my right knee somehow banged up against a step of the ladder, which forced my body to lose its balance. Sweat dripped from my hands as I held on to the handles for dear life. Behind my sunglasses was the definition of fear written in my eyes. After several motivational thoughts and deep breaths, I continued to climb. I got my two feet on solid ground and was forced to admit I was not okay. My body was trying to tell me something and thought it was a good idea to react in the middle of an ocean where the nearest medical center is hundreds of miles away. I wobbled over to sit down by my friends on the bench. My mom and my brother sat across me, and my dad decided to stay on the lower level of the boat. Everyone was laughing and having a blast as I sat on the bench terrified, thinking that this may be the end. I closed my eyes for a couple of seconds and tried to open them back up. It is such a simple physical action, to open up our eyes, and I struggled to do such a simple act. I could hear my friends ask me questions, but I could not respond because I then lost strength to communicate. Every muscle started tingling as if energy were releasing from my body.

Moments go by, and I began to lose my hearing. The energy sensation just kept getting stronger and stronger. *My body is under attack*, I kept thinking to myself. *What do I do to stop it?* It took everything out of me to squint my eyes just a tiny bit in order to see my mom's lips move. I couldn't hear her, but I could read her lips, and they read, "Jess, are you okay?"

That was the last thing I remember.

Just like that, my physical body collapsed, and I ended up on top of my friend like a dead weight. One of the dads we were with was a doctor, so he lowered me to the ground. They called my name, but I did not answer. Everyone surrounded me, just praying I wake up or give them a sign on what to do. My body lay there for two and a half minutes with no heartbeat. My family and friends were living in the moment of shock and fear. My mom was crying, my brother was covering his eyes, my friends were in shock, and my dad was on the lower level hearing the commotion from up top, wondering what was going on. (I only know this because I asked after the incident.)

I, on the other hand, was in a different world. It was bright. I have never felt so at peace and comfortable. Shining yellow. This energy was joyful, happy, and was the core of the sun. I felt strong. My scars were no longer weak, and I felt so large, almost another version of coming alive. I was so at peace I thought I was sleeping in my comfy bed. All I could hear was ringing in my ears, but it has a graceful ring to it. My soul left my body, and to this day, I have never felt so free.

People ask if it was heaven I went to or if I saw people. I do not know where I went, but I do know that I was safe, loved, and complete. My soul was at home.

The yellow presence started to fade, and I fought to stay there. I did not want to leave this paradise. I felt my soul leaving its home and returning to this world. The floor was cold, and I became aware of my toes, fingertips, and nose. I smelled the fishy ocean and knew I was not in paradise. Selfishly, I did not want to open my eyes.

But then my mom's cry registered in my brain, and my heart started beating again. I opened up my eyes, and I kid you not, it was a scene out of a movie. All I could see were heads surrounding me with fear in their eyes. They did not know what to do with me.

They offered me help, but I refused. I got on my two feet after I drank orange juice and looked around. I was the girl to "pray for," "center of attention," "miracle," "charity case." I put my sunglasses back on and said, "My name is Jessica Helene Zacharias. I am a junior in high school, and I just fainted. We are on a boat to swim with the stingrays." The passengers on board starting clapping as if I just acted out a scene from a play. However, it did not come present to me until years later in which that specific scene stands as my door to what would be to the beginning of my journey to spiritual growth.

My dad and I made the decision I should get out of the sun and go rest. In order to do that, I had to climb down the ladder, which literally just took my breath away and walk by all the passengers on the boat. Behind my sunglasses, I felt the stares of worry, sadness, and fear. All I wanted to do was run away and hide in a corner all by myself. We ventured off the boat, got on the bus, and got on another boat to get to the cruise ship, and each time, I was faced with the question, "Hi, ma'am, how are you doing today?"

Silent and visible tears turned into an inward and physical waterfall. I was scared, upset, embarrassed, and angry. I did not understand what happened. I did not know if I should explain to my parents or friends where I went or how free I felt or how I wanted to stay there or how I was afraid to even breathe because something bad could happen.

When my dad and I got back to the cruise ship, I sprinted toward my bed and collapsed again. Just sobbing. I walked and stared at myself in the mirror and did not know who I was even looking at. Or in fact, what I was even looking at.

It was time for dinner, which meant it was time to stand and walk as the center of attention.

"Pick out a cute dress, put some makeup on, and pretend it never happened" were the thoughts that ran through my head. If we just forget it did not happen, I would not have to face my fear of being the girl who needs assistance because she is not strong enough.

Short term, it worked. Long term, not so much. I thought I was protecting myself and being strong when I was actually doing the opposite. I became someone who lived two lives. One that did everything for everyone but never got close enough to show who I really am. I was afraid to show my not-so-pretty side because I was afraid of being made fun of. Not being accepted. Like, who my age would understand or even be able to relate to the idea of my soul leaving my body and I stood face-to-face with the core of the sun/

God? Which is why my fight to be normal and not letting my journey truly shine has been the hardest battle I have ever fought.

When I am by myself, I think and talk out loud. I knew what I had experienced does not really happen to normal people. I wanted an answer or a reason. Not to brag about it—but to know why it happened and how I can share my experience with others. I wanted to make the right action with the story because ever since that moment, the higher power, the angels, the Lord, and the universe and I have a special bond that continues to grow every step of my journey. Without them, I am not complete. I am not the Jessica Zacharias people know without their love and guidance. They are loyal to me, and as their friend, sharing knowledge from them is an honor.

For a while, I believed the color yellow would symbolize my moment in time when I experienced the outside world with the angels and the higher power. Exactly four years later, the color yellow appeared again in my journey with more meaning and power than ever before.

Stranded Island

Dealing with my out-of-body experience, yes, it opened up my spirituality, but I became more fearful than ever. I also had to go through many tests to figure out as to why I had that episode. Turns out, I have a hole in my heart—a heart murmur—and my arteries leak. It is called pulmonary stenosis, and my blood was not flowing properly through my heart. Is it life-threatening? No, but it is something that needs care or else it could turn life-threatening. Awesome.

Knowing that I am different and somehow connected to the universe in a strange way and holding fear in the idea of trust meant keeping a healthy friendship was always a challenge. I mean, it is no one's fault, but no one was ever on the same page as me. I never understood on how I was always the one getting hurt. My mother always told me they were envious of me. She would tell me this when I stood alone in a parking lot waiting for my friends, just to find out that they all went to another party and did not invite me. She would tell me this when people would make statements like I am too sensitive or I am a walking charity case. She would tell me this when no one remembered my birthday in high school even though I threw many surprise birthday parties for everyone. She would remind me about the life aspect of hard times every time tears streamed down my broken face. Along with challenging times, she would tell me that no matter how hard I try to express my thoughts and feelings, no one would ever understand where I am coming from. She would explain to me on how my life is different from everyone else's and how I must accept that, how I am on a different realm of life compared to individuals my age. No matter how lonely, hurtful, and frustrating my journey may be, there is still a reason to smile and enjoy life. Be the bigger person, let it go, and move forward. One day they will learn, but that is the path they must go on. "Focus on your journey, and your time will come," she would say.

I never questioned my mother, but I honestly never understood what she meant. The thoughts in my head would consist of "Why on earth would they be envious of me? Do they realize how every day is a miracle, and in order to keep on living I must fight adversity every moment of my life?"

Overtime, I became a pro at putting on a strong face and building tough skin. My counselor brought up the idea that I am a victim of my own actions, and honestly, he is right. Shining light wherever I would go became my unpaid job. I would go out of my way to make others happy. Instead of focusing on my mind, body, and soul, I was focusing on others. Yes, it is important to help others and share love for everyone who crosses your journey. However, loving, accepting, and taking care of yourself is the foundation for living the best life you possibly can. Life just teaches you those lessons in the strangest ways, like having you stand alone in a parking lot waiting for your peers.

Showing people the side of darkness rarely happened because I did everything in my power to control it. The mind-set I created is that if I could be the person everyone could lean on, I would not have to worry about my own problems. My problems were too big for me to handle, let alone share them with people who do not understand, I would think to myself. Teenage years—so enjoyable.

It was my senior year in high school, and not going to lie, I was ready to get out. Yes, it had its moments like senior spring break, prom, Halloween, football games, and the all-night party, but it was time.

I was eager to venture to the new chapter and see what it would bring. Our graduation ceremony ironically was held at the college campus I was going to attend that upcoming fall. A day before graduation, I found out I made the athletics dance team, so the O'rena (place I was graduating in) served as more than just my graduation stage: it served as my new foundation for my journey at Oakland.

Summer flew by, and all my friends and I said our final see-you-laters. No one knew what to expect, but we knew it was going to be eventful. I kept in decent contact with my friends. I learned during this time on how everyone is on their own yellow brick road and how you just have to accept it.

The car was packed, and my family was emotional! It was time for me to move into my dorm on campus. My roommate was a little wishy-washy, but I did not want to judge too soon. As my family and I were unpacking, she never showed up. I called her and texted her, but she did not respond until the next day. I thought it was strange but did not think too much about it. Plus, I already had some friends to hang out with, so I was not too worried.

The next day she showed up with a microwave and her pillow. She was tall, very skinny, and dark-haired. I introduced myself, and she seemed reserved. For the next couple of hours, I tried starting a conversation with her, but it was not going so well. I noticed she had a tattoo on her back near her shoulder, so I asked her about it. She looked at me and responded, "Do you really want to know?" I was stunned as to how rude she responded, but I insisted if she did not want to share, she did not have to.

Turns out, she has a daughter and gave it up for adoption. Yep, at this point, I kind of regretted asking the question. What do you say to that? So being the therapist that I am, I created a comfortable environment for her to share her story. An hour later, I heard about how her relationship with the baby's father and the adoptive parents. This moment created a soft spot for her in my heart.

It was later on during the semester that the soft spot became a ring of fire. I would wake up in the morning and see not one but two naked bodies in her bed. Each night was a different guy. Sometimes she would be gone for days—even weeks—and then return back without even acknowledging how abnormal her behavior was.

After class, I would come home to her blasting her music, drinking a fifth that was sitting on her desk. I had no idea what to do. I tried everything in my power to make the place feel like home. I went out and bought a new futon and pillows. I set it up so that it looked welcoming and friendly.

The next morning I came back from class, and I walk in to her being intimate with a guy on my new futon. I was livid and felt betrayed. How could she ever, in a million years, have the nerve to do such a thing? I was jealous of hearing about all my other friends and how they loved their roommates. Once again, I stood alone on my island praying for a break.

Halfway through the first semester, she started smoking in the room. I asked her if she would not mind moving locations to smoke, and that is when the disaster party began. We ended up having to have a meeting with our RA, and she had nothing but negative and disgusting words to say to me. I closed my eyes and went to my happy place.

I then looked at my RA and said, "Clearly, this is a relationship not good or healthy for both of us. I will move rooms by tomorrow morning."

My roommate was appalled by my remark and did not understand how I remained calm, which, honestly, I was thinking the same thing. She got up out of the chair and said, "That is it. I am moving out." Since that moment, I never saw her again. Typical Jessica moment.

Learning to be Comfortable
with the Uncomfortable

"Do you know your mommy's phone number?" the cop asked in a baby's voice.

"Yes, I actually do. Give me the phone," I confidently responded as I sat in the backseat of a cop car.

It was my first weekend of college, and I end up in the back of a cop car. So much for being rebellious and a typical college student.

That night was the night teens look forward to. Freedom from the parents, new relationship flings, and blowing up Instagram. My friends and I were celebrating just like every other college student in the world. It was welcome week—meaning, it was expected to start off the semester with a bang. This night determined how your social life would be. In our generation, if we don't make something of ourselves that night, our value on the social pole travels to the bottom.

Since I physically cannot vomit, it puts limits on my party life. Not entirely an awful thing in the long run, but I stand out. I am either the mother of the party or the one people are taking care of, which usually is the mother because we all know how I feel about showing weakness.

I will admit it: I poured myself way too much to drink. The drink was too good not to drink though.

But all I fought for my entire life was to be normal like everyone else. These new friends didn't know much about my health story. They had an idea but didn't realize how serious it can be, so the "freedom" aspect of the night held a higher meaning then just from my parents. I was finally free from my struggle that created deep wounds that turned into scars.

Alcohol and the half of the stomach I have left do not mix. Malibu, peach Smirnoff, and orange juice do though. You know the term blacking out in reference to drinking? Well, ironically enough, I happened to be the walking definition of that phrase.

I woke up with a deep blood-gushing wound on top of my ankle. Great, another scar, I thought to myself. The gray ceiling was what I saw when I opened up my eyes. My heavy head made a dent in my foam pillow, but I was in my bed, so I was all safe—at least that was what I assumed.

By this time, the alcohol has worn off, but it was still in my system. Then the nightmare happened.

After three obnoxious knocks on my dorm door, I heard, "Police, open up."

It had to be a joke. I have never been the one to have a negative relationship with the police. I was the kid who would go to school then go to the hospital where nurses served as my friends and the ugly gowns were my wardrobe. Yes, I drank some my senior year of high school but never to the point where I got in trouble with the cops. I was screwed. My bed was lofted, so I tried to remain calm as I climbed down my ladder to open the door.

My foot missed the first step on the ladder, which then led me to miss all the steps, so I ended up falling six feet to the ground. The whole dorm shook. As I tumbled down, my head banged the wall, and I landed on my knees.

Target's $10 mirror I purchased was shattered into a million pieces since it was on the wall my head decided to get close with. I saw with my two brown eyes the reflection of my life in a million pieces: broken, shattered, and full of scars.

I wanted to scream, cry, and run. Instead, I told myself the next time I would look in the mirror, I would see a strong lady who turned her broken, shattered, full-of-scars life into a story worth telling. Not really sure where this notion of building inner strength came from. But it did.

I pulled myself together and opened the door, keeping cool as three cops were standing in my front of my dorm, and I was respectful since I knew they were just doing their jobs.

As I blew into the breathalyzer, the female cop noticed my medical bracelet on my right wrist.

She then proceeded to whisper into another cop's ear about what she observed.

My life turned from a typical-college-student moment into a medical emergency. I was a candidate that they believed needed assistance, and if something were to happen to me, their jobs would be on the line. In just four hours, my titles changed from "normal free Jess" to "the girl who needs help."

Wonderful, just wonderful, I thought to myself.

They took me to the back of a cop car even though I was walking fine. Well, I think I was. Anyway, I was sitting on a bench in the police station waiting for my parents. Not one tear shed because anger filled my heart, body, and soul. Anger on why it had to happen to me. Anger because I just wanted *one* night to fit in. That was all I was asking for. But no, I ended up in the back of a cop car flashing its red, white, and blue colors.

I committed a crime by drinking under age and received an MIP (for those who aren't familiar, minor in possession). Drinking under age.

Once I saw my parents, I lost it. I could not control my tears or screams. My dad couldn't understand what I was saying, so he went back in to ask what the story was and how it happened. When we got home, I ran to my room and wept. By this time, I was sober, and I knew exactly what happened. My mom came into my room and lay with me until I fell asleep.

Ever since that night, I put my medical bracelet in my wallet. I was livid, not at the cop but at my eventful life that always had to take a different turn. By hiding my bracelet, I was hiding a part of me that, at the time, I despised.

Those next nine months, I hid. I never went to a party, went out, or enjoyed myself. Wait—that is a lie. I went to one party with my dance team friends, and the cheerleaders took a picture of us and sent it to our coach, so we ended up getting in more trouble. But besides that one night, I didn't deserve to be happy. I was throwing a pity party for myself. Disappointment controlled my life. I disappointed my Lord, my parents, my friends, but most importantly, I was disappointed in myself. My anger sat on my stomach like glue. Once it hardened, it stuck. *I know I can't drink that much. Why did I hurt myself?* I kept thinking. I was better than that. The glue just kept getting harder and harder.

When I thought it would get a little easier, it got worse. It was the day of my sentencing, and my emotions were raw. The car ride to the court was nothing but silence. Once the car was parked, my parents and I walked in through security and up the stairs down a long hallway. Once we turned the corner, I saw with my own eyes what category of humans I was being categorized to. One by one, attorneys or lawyers showed up, and my parents and I patiently waited for mine before we would make our way into the courtroom. He never showed. So what does that mean? It meant that the person I trusted to guide me and help me left me standing in front of the judge all by myself. Once again alone.

The system was controlled to the tee, from who had the authority to open the door to when could the door be opened to when we all rise and when we all sit down. It bugged the crap out of me. One by one, individuals went up and confessed their crime. Innocent Jessica though everyone was there for an MIP, but I was wrong. I saw a female get taken away from her family, placed in handcuffs, and thrown into jail. I saw a male get sentenced to prison as his family wept. I had no idea that this was a part of this world that happens every single day.

Finally, it was my turn.

All eyes joined together as I stood up and walked to the podium without showing weakness. *Must show strength*, I thought. Don't show you are weak even though my soul was weeping. The courage to speak to the judge felt as if I was learning to speak for the very first time.

Then my mom stood up and walked up next to me at the stand. He asked if I had an attorney but my mom played the role. It was a moment where I felt loved. I wasn't alone. I pleaded guilty and confessed I made a mistake.

Money fines were absolutely insane and made a dent in my wallet and in my parents' wallet too. Had to pay for an alcohol counselor, probation fees each month, and criminal fines.

Community service was a part of my probation. Volunteered at an old person's home. It was similar to lifetime fitness or a gym.

I worked the pool and tennis desk. Even though I was there for probation, I surprisingly enjoyed myself. I adore old people because their stories are beautiful to hear. All they want is an ear to listen to the advice they kept inside. So that was what I did, provided the ear to listen, but little did they know their words were the wisdom I needed to hear.

Being on probation, I was not allowed to leave the state without permission. Before my family traveled to Indiana for my cousin's grad party, I had to get approved by the court. The process was completed, but the compromise was I had to go to the nearest jail and take the breathalyzer test every morning. It was that or wear a tether around my foot noticeable for the world to see. I chose jail.

Each morning my mom and I woke up before the sunrise. It was summertime, so I was wearing shorts, sunglasses, and a tank top. We pulled up to a green brick building. The car was parked, and it was time to witness a jail atmosphere.

My legs were out of the car when I noticed how terrifying the next half hour was going to be. Along the green brick building were windows that had silver cages and bars boxed around them. Criminals were behind those bars. I slowly get out of the car, and I made eye contact with the color orange. Each individual who was in jail was grabbing on to the bars from the inside to get a view of me. I was an object to them. Every movement I made was being observed. I felt sick to my stomach I wanted to puke, but that is something I couldn't escape from.

Then just as I started blowing into the breathalyzer test, sirens went off. They were releasing the criminals and taking them to their community service.

"A bus is transporting them, so don't worry. You are fine right here," the cop told me in a calm voice because I'm sure he could feel the nervous energy from my body.

One by one, they walked right past me, checking me out up and down with their hands in handcuffs and chains dragging from their feet. Times like these, you wish you can fast-forward, but no, they happen in slow motion. No matter where I looked, someone was staring at me. The cop who was testing me even told them to look away.

Finally, I was done, and I walked with a purpose to the car, slammed the door, and put my seatbelt on, staring ahead.

"You okay?" my mom asked.

"I'm fine," I answered confidently even though the truth showed behind my sunglasses. As the tears streamed down my face, I turned to look out the window so I could hide my pain again.

A positive of my medical history at the time was the action of peeing in a cup. It is an action I am a professional at. It was a Wednesday when I got called in to pee in a cup. I pulled up and parked my car, observed the situation, and couldn't believe what I had to do.

I was wearing tight leggings, boots, sunglasses, and the brightest pink jacket I owned. Not that bad, right? Typical girl outfit. The realization I made was this: Out of twenty people in line, I was the only female. Once again, I fell underneath the object category.

My chin was to my chest, sunglasses on, and pretending I was on the phone with someone—until some guy came up to me and started flirting. The problem was that I really couldn't escape. Then more guys surrounded me, and I became the center of attention. Feeling the stares as they rank my ass was my last straw. I closed my eyes to hold back the tears. I stood helpless and alone.

"Jessica Zacharias," the cop announced in a loud, deep voice.

Did you really have to shout my name that loud?

I shut the door and pulled my pants down to pee in the cup. My pants were down, and the door swung open. Open for all the men in line to see. I was demanded to stop. A witness must be in the bathroom with the criminal to confirm it is indeed their pee.

Cue all the emotions that fall under the embarrassment category.

I peed in the cup as a worker watched me, pulled my pants up, washed my hands, and made sure I left nothing behind.

I got in my car, locked the doors twice, buckled my seatbelt, and hurried as fast as I could to get out of there. As I was driving, the familiar tears behind the sunglasses started to create the waterfall.

During this time, I was not proud of whom I was becoming. I hid in my room every weekend, or I went back home because I was too embarrassed to show my face to own up to what I did and why I did it. People think I drank to just have fun, but I drank to fit in. Especially in college, it is everywhere. I wanted to experience college like normal people do. But then again, life showed me how I am not supposed to be "normal."

My friendships were not as strong and healthy as they should be during this time of challenge. How could I be someone's friend when I could not even look at the mirror without seeing a stranger? The idea of control bothered me. I would get upset if the dishes were not clean or if someone did not throw the garbage away.

The dance team I was on was a unique one. My coach, at the time, was very demanding and controlling. The team years before I even attended college decided not to act so classy, which meant dance team was on probation. This really bugged me because athletics did not even know who this new team was, but we had to deal with the consequences of the previous team. This meant no eye contact with any athletes, no drinking or partying, no becoming friends with anyone in athletics. Literally controlled my life. I would purposely walk the other way if I saw an athlete come near me or let someone cut in front of me in line if I was standing too close to an athlete. I became my own worst enemy because I was letting people control my eyes on how I view this world.

The amount of stress my body felt was unbearable. I was afraid and sensitive to every little thing. People would ask me how my day was, and I would flashback to my morning standing in the criminal line to pay my fees. Just thinking of the thought and the process to open up to someone about what was really going on was like scratching my fingernails on a chalkboard.

For my probation, I did have to see an alcoholic counselor because the city I was charged in thought I was an alcoholic. Little did they know alcohol traumatized me, so I opened up to my counselor a lot about my thoughts and behaviors about the idea of alcohol.

"How can I have such a huge criminal offense when it was one mistake and the people that charged me with it do not even know who I really am?" I would exclaim. He then changed his body in his chair, leaned forward with his hands together, and asked, "Do you know who you are and who you want to be?"

As some dear friends of mine would say, that moment was a game-changer for my mental strength during that time of my journey.

After a long year, it was time for the court to let me be free.

Shoulders were back, chin was lifted, smile was bright as I wrote my name down on the probation sign-in sheet one last time. By this time, I knew everyone there by name. But I went there knowing it was my last time ever dealing with the court system, especially this specific court, or the hellhole as I like to refer to it as. Did my business, waved to the police who stood guarding the doors, and danced my way out to my car with the weight lifted off my shoulders—I did it! I was finally free.

As I was driving out of the parking lot, I said, "It was nice knowing ya! Thanks for all the wonderful memories, but I am not upset that I will never see you ever again."

A year and a half later, I would sit less than ten feet away from a murder in that same hellhole I thought I was done with.

Eyewitness

When I was born, the doctors told my parents that it would not be surprising if I had a difficult connection with them because of the trauma I experienced. They wished my parents luck on raising me and made it clear I would have developmental issues. It was my parents' goal not to make that happen, not to make me "normal" but to treat me like every parent should with unconditional love, respect, and trust. My parents are two of the strongest individuals I have ever known. Through the fights, tears, and counseling, they made it through because, think about it, I was the baby that came into this world that brought the unknown. Not many people discuss what steps to take when your child is sick and who only has a couple of years to live. My parents' relationship took its own journey down the growth yellow brick road.

If it wasn't for my mom and her determination to prove the doctors wrong, I don't know if I would be here today writing a book. She has always been my hero. My days were not complete without talking to her every single day. She was my best friend, and I would do anything for her. She has this special vibe that makes her Helene Zacharias. All my friends loved her and would tell her things that sometimes I did not even know. Plus, she can read right through people. So there was no bullshitting around with Mrs. Z.

Growing up, my dad always worked. He was always at sporting events or dance competitions on the weekends, but during the week, we hardly saw him. Not his fault at all, but that is how the cards were drawn. I held in a lot of my anger about the situation because he would come home and act like nothing was wrong even though my brother and I witnessed how it affected my mother. Some days we were fine, but others days she wept. She cried because she wanted him home. She wanted to go to family parties with the whole family. She worked so late by the time she got home my brother and I would be off doing our own things, which meant we all ate alone. With this dynamic, my brother, my mom, and I became a team. Someone would get the mail, cut the grass, make dinner, and do the dishes. Yes, some days I opted out of doing a chore, which does not fly with my mother, which I learned very quickly.

When my dad came home, he always had to be in charge. I guess he was trying to make up for lost time and wanted to feel included in family decisions and behaviors. On days when we all were happy, we ate together and went around the table saying one positive thing about our day. I was young at the time and wanted to be close with my dad because I knew he loved me very much. It pulled at my heart how I could ever be angry with him, but I knew it was something I had to work on. The idea that he would be gone for weeks on end frightened me. If you ask my family, we all would say we definitely are unique. I thought my family was put through enough with my whole journey and my dad's job. But I was young and being naïve. What happened next was somehow a brutal, dark, rock-bottom blessing. Well, at least that is how I look at it.

It was the summer of 2008 when we were trying to take a family picture at the beach in California when my mom looked like she was drunk trying to walk on the sand. Her ankles kept giving out, and we all brushed it off and laughed because she was making a fool out of herself. Ironically enough, that was our first sign to get ready to experience the journey as a family to live our lives on no so solid ground.

I did not really become aware of my mom getting sick until my senior year of high school. Similar to my belief that everyone went to the hospital after school, I thought it was normal for moms to always be going to the doctors. She never made a big deal about it though.

I remember not hearing about an appointment until weeks after, which really pissed me off. How could we grow as a family when my brother and I are not aware of the truth? She would always say, "Do not worry, I will be fine."

My mom's body started to go through some drastic changes. She cut back on junk and tried to work out, but her body kept getting bigger and bigger. She became very emotional and sensitive. Honestly, I thought she was going through menopause at a young age. But that was not the case. Similar to my health journey, my mom's is also very rare and unique in its own way.

Each year she got a different diagnosis. One year it was diabetes, another was the fear of breast cancer, the other year was shingles, lymphedema, fibromyalgia, and the list goes on and on.

Not many doctors knew what to do with her. Heck, she did not even know what to think, feel, or even begin to understand why she has been sick for so long.

I was sitting alone at a Starbucks doing my homework like a good student would when I got a call January of 2013—the call society warns you about, the call that changed my life forever.

My mom did not have to say much for me to know what was going on.

A brain tumor—how do you even handle something like this? My body went into shock and protection, which was not good for anyone who came my way. I could not lose my mom at the age of nineteen, so I put on my big girl armor and suited up for battle.

The tumor sat on her pituitary gland, which controls your hormones. Makes complete sense on why she was feeling the way she was.

"How is your mom doing?" is a question that unfortunately has been formed into my everyday life. You would think it would get easier to respond, but ironically enough, it got harder because every time I was asked, society was slapping me across the face with the fact that my mother has not gotten better. Now I understand people were looking out for me and actually do care for my family, but boy was that question an emotional trigger.

When news of the tumor was announced, yes, I suited up for battle, but I prayed that an end was near. I was hopeful that she would fight through, that God would be on my family's side and cure my mom.

Needless to say, a new journey was just unfolding with more challenges and much more fear for everyone involved.

Who really has control?

A life motto I have is "Take life day by day because you never know what can happen next." Cheesy, yes, but it is the truth. My sophomore year of college was coming to an end, dance team was starting to die down, and summer was just around the corner. Plus, my birthday was at the end of the month, so I was ecstatic to finally see the light at the end of the tunnel.

It was April Fool's Day when, ironically enough, my journey played a prank on me. There was something special about that day. The sun was shining bright, the sky was bright blue, and the clouds were full. I had an appointment with a dear friend who I connect with really well on a soul level. She has always motivated me to be the best I can be, and whenever I see her, I am on cloud nine. Granted, she is in her late fifties, but I am an old soul that connects with people of all ages. My attitude was bubbly and peachy. In ways, I felt really alive and well. I ate dinner with a friend who was more like a sister to me. Since I was in the why-not mood, I ordered some warm chicken fingers and fries. Boy, was it tasty. As we were leaving, I started to hiccup, and I joked, "Oh, it is going to be a long night tonight!"

She knew about my esophagus and how when I burp, all hell breaks loose, but we just let it go and went for a drive. She dropped me off at my apartment, and since no one was there, I did my own thing. I got in the shower, reminiscing about my happy day, singing and dancing in the shower. Before I could comprehend, I was lying flat on the ground looking up as the water poured over me. I lay naked on my shower floor confused as to what just happened. My eyes wandered in a panic to see if there was any blood around me, but what I noticed was that my stomach was expanding, and it was not stopping. I wanted to scream for help, but that would be a waste of energy since no one was even home. I got on all fours and crawled out of the shower, grabbed a towel, reached for my phone, and let the shower run since I was too weak to stand. I looked at my phone and stared at it. My family was on a cruise for the week for my brother's spring break. Who do I call? Do I call someone to help me? Or do I just deal with it by myself? Do I become vulnerable so others can see a side of me that I am not fully willing to show?

These thoughts were running through my mind as I was hugging the toilet and getting up close and personal with it for about twenty minutes. My body was not getting any better, I was actually getting worse. It took a while, but I got over the fear of being vulnerable and called my friend who I had dinner with. I told her it was not a joke, and I needed some serious help. Poor girl, I probably traumatized her. It is kind of humorous actually. I have that effect on people. I either traumatize them or enlighten them. Sometimes both happen even.

At the time, she lived in the same apartment complex, so she arrived fairly quickly. I turned off the shower, got my blanket and pillow, put some clothes on, and camped out in the bathroom. When she arrived, her eyes grew wide, and she said, "Jess, I know you don't want to, but I think it is time to go to the hospital." I knew she was right; I was stubborn to believe it. I hesitated and just thought to myself, *Great, my parents are going to come home in a couple of days and ask me how my week was, and I have to tell them I went to the hospital.* Typical Jessica moment.

After I let my ego have its play day, I agreed it would be the best solution. Grabbed my blanket, my slippers, and my little stuffed dog, Lucky. We got in the car, and we were off to the hospital.

It was late at night, so not that many cars were out and about. As my blanket wrapped around me, my slippers keeping my feet warm, and Lucky in my hands, I gazed out the window. I thought to myself, *What is the purpose behind this moment? I do not know if I could do this.* I did not feel like being the warrior. Ironically enough, the song "Anything Could Happen" by Ellie Goulding started playing on the radio. I then giggled and said to myself, "Okay, I will go with it."

One of my favorite aspects about my story is that just by looking at me, you would have no idea of all the challenges my body has gone through. The receptionist probably thought she was getting pranked when I insisted I was there because I could not puke. She said, "Honey, the bathroom is right over there. Let me know if you need anything."

I giggled and responded in gratitude but then continued to talk. As soon as I said I was born with TEF and I have a rope in my stomach which does not allow me to physically vomit, she immediately ran, grabbed a wheelchair, and rushed me into the emergency room to see the doctor as if I were a celebrity or something.

From that point, I was treated like royalty. Because of HIPPA violations, I had to explain how it was okay for my friend to be in the room as they took care of me. To this day, she is the first person to actually witness me having a medical episode besides my family. Just in a matter of an hour, I went from calm, accepting Jess to barely even walk or keep my eyes open Jess. As I walked to the bathroom down the hall, I nearly collapsed and desperately hung on to the wall handle and used everything in me to get back up. Nurses ran and assisted me as I made my way to the bathroom. My body was resisting all the scans and tests that were performed, which meant the next step was to stick a tube up my nose down to my stomach.

Well, people, they do not put you out for this kind of stuff. I was so frightened, anxious, and angry. I cried and cried because I was embarrassed and angry that it actually had to happen. I was so little when I would have tubes up my nose that I forgot how it felt. A part of me died inside when the nurse walked in with the tube in her hands. It was as long as me. My friend grabbed my hand and started rubbing my forehead. I just looked at her and hollered.

My emotions were high, and the first time, I slapped the nurse across the face because I was in so much pain. If any of you have ever had to get a tube up your nose, which then travels down your throat into your stomach, you would understand the willingness to holler or even feel the need to protect yourself. We agreed that I needed to time to relax, and they gave me ten minutes to breathe.

My eyes closed tightly as they could as the tube went up. The tube scratched the back of my throat, and my body instantly started rejecting it. When my body rejects stuff, I flop around like a fish out of water. Farting, or even worse, I poop my pants. No wonder I have control issues; having no control over your body is the scariest feeling.

When nurses have a mission, they will do whatever to accomplish it. With my body rejecting the tube, they did not let that stop them. "All done," the nurses rejoiced as the tube sat in place. "Now you have to wait half an hour with it in, and then we will take it out."

A half hour! Are you kidding me? When a tube is in your body, let alone your nose and throat, normal everyday motions became uncomfortably painful.

A baseball game was on, so I tried to focus on watching that to take the pain away. I was in shock that my friend was still there by my side and accepting this side of me. She was making me laugh and made the atmosphere comfortable. Even though I felt safe, that half hour felt like ten years. By the last five minutes, I was turning into a crabby bitch. The tube travels near the eyes so even if you do not want to shed a tear, you automatically do. The waterfall poured uncontrollably as soon as the nurses started pulling it out.

Before I knew it, the nurses put their hands gently on my bed handles and said, "We have to admit you, Jessica."

"Admit me? No! That is not happening!" I screamed.

"We know you want to go home, but it would be best for you to stay here, especially since your parents are traveling and you would be by yourself. You may need to get scoped," they explained.

"Scoped? As in surgery?" I screamed even louder.

"That is a possibility. The doctor will be doing rounds early tomorrow morning, and we will know more then," they explained as they were walking out of the room.

What has my life come to? I thought. I was sleep-deprived and just wanted to go back to the place where I was surrounded with yellow light.

It was around four in the morning, so I insisted that my friend could go back home and get some sleep because we both had school the next day.

In my opinion, hospitals or care centers need to fix their ceilings or add some flavor to them. As the patient lying in a moving bed, there is nowhere else to look except up. Yes, the shining yellow bright lights are fun to look at, but they are boring. We need some pictures or some quotes to read as we make our way through the hospital tied to a hospital bed with nowhere to go.

We arrived on the admitting floor, and I was forced into the room. Nurses were lined up waiting for me as I sarcastically smiled and introduced myself. I held it together for the most part until they asked where my family was. I wished they were with me, but God had a reason for not having me go on the trip with them. Once the nurses left and I was all alone lying on a hospital bed with the lights off, I thought to myself, *This is not happening.* Then I started laughing because who am I kidding? Of course, this would happen to me. The laughing turned into tears and self-doubt. I was trapped with no unlock key in sight.

I knew I had to call someone from my family, so I called my grandma. She rushed to the hospital and was in disbelief.

Living as a chronically ill patient, I pick up on many hospital codes and signals. I overheard the nurses and doctor discussing my case. He walked in and insisted he would get me better. It is funny because when it comes to doctors and nurses putting their hands on my body, I hardly flinch. Maybe I became numb to it. But when friends or family want to hug me, I flinch.

I needed to get scoped, which meant I made the big girl decision without talking to my parents about being put under.

But of course, the day would not be completed without a Jessica moment. On my way to the surgical room, I received a phone call. At the time, I was applying for internships through school, and I applied at a local news station. When I answered the phone, I was unsure on what they were going to say, but she asked if it was a good time to talk. I didn't even think twice, and I said yes, it was even though I was literally on a hospital bed in the hallway on my way to get surgery—I crack myself up sometimes. She explained to tell me that I made it through the first round, and it was time to set up an interview date. The nurses and doctors were at a standstill just waiting for me to finish my phone call. I scheduled the interview date, thanked the supervisor, and hung up the phone with pride. I gave my phone to a nurse and said, "Okay, people, let's do this." Five minutes later, I was out.

When I woke up from surgery, I felt sore and weak. I am always clear that I love orange popsicles and a warm blanket when I wake up. My small intestine was inflamed. However, they were curious as to why. For the next couple of days, I was on the ice diet—could not eat anything except ice. What a delicious five-star course meal.

Yeah, that made me one happy camper. But after a couple of days, I got used to it. The support and love I received that week was incredible. My nurses allowed my visitors to stay as long as they wanted. Someone was always in my room, and I will be forever grateful. College friends, dance friends, teammates, students, family friends, and even some of my dance teachers came to visit me. My grandma would come and stop by. She is known for bringing me goodies and yummy food, but since I could only eat ice, it was a problem. When my grandpa came, he brought me the *New York Times* just so that I would be in the loop.

But the friend who promised she would be with me every step of the way, indeed, did do that. She would go to school and then we would color. This is when I learned the importance of art therapy. It was nice because when I was alone at night, I would color pictures, and it would take my mind off why I was in the hospital. I made sure to share the art by coloring pictures for my nurses as a way of giving back.

It was now Thursday night, and I was getting antsy. I was ready to leave. My grandparents joked about how they would not be surprised if they turned on the news and saw a story about how a hospital patient escaped. The thought about how much schoolwork I was missing, the thought of missing my job and being controlled by the hospital was no longer fun. I kept bugging my nurses for them to release me, but they couldn't. Why? Because I needed to show them that I could poop, and I needed to walk at least ten laps around the hospital floor a day. Sounds easy, right? But let me tell you, when your body is not in its happy place, pooping is challenging to do and walking one lap is similar to a marathon.

My left arm was going numb because that is the arm that had the IV in it. When an IV is in your arm, the range of motion your arm can do is slim to none. My whole body was losing mobility, I could not even stand straight in the shower for that long of a time, so my new normal of a shower was rinsing myself in the sink.

As I would do my laps, I would chat with other patients and discover their stories. I would help them find the positive and show them that they have the light that this world needs. Once I was done being the peacemaker on the hospital floor, I would walk near the end of the hallway to look out the window. The message of how anything could happen and you must be grateful for everything that is in your journey came to life. I wanted to walk outside, sit by a tree, and just enjoy the birds' chirping. I would be lying if I didn't share that thoughts did cross my mind about what would happen if I just jumped out of the window since I felt the whole universe was against me.

It was time to go to bed, and I still did not have idea on when I would be able to go home. I prayed for the first time. Praying always made me feel good, but I never know if I do it right or not. I grew up Catholic, but to be honest, I knew it was not for me. Every Sunday, we would go to church; and I would never feel good about this one priest, but everyone loved him, so I just went with it. Fast-forward to a couple of years later, news was released that he embezzled hundreds of thousands of dollars from the church. My intuition was right. I lost faith after that story came out and especially lost it during my time on probation. I knew it was time to release that anger and start believing in something again because I hit my rock bottom. I bowed my head, closed my eyes, and began weeping, explaining that I knew this was happening for a reason, but could you give me guidance on what I am supposed to do next?

What happened next gave me chills.

After I was done talking to God, the divine and the higher power, I listened to music and fell asleep with no pain. It was the first time since I was admitted that I got some decent amount of sleep, except the fact that every two hours, my nurses would come and poke me in the stomach with a shot to make sure my blood flows properly so I would not get a blood clot and die.

As I was enjoying my slumber, one of my nurses woke me up. She said, "I am sorry, angel, and I know you won't be happy, but we have to switch rooms. We have to move you now."

I looked at her with the sassiest look on my face. I thought she was joking until she started taking my pictures and get-well cards down.

"It's four in the morning! Can't I move rooms when the doctor does his rounds at 8:00 a.m.?" I pleaded.

The answer was no.

Forty-five minutes later, I am finally getting settled into my new room. By this time, I was wide awake, so I started to color. Once the light shine in the room, I realized I had a roommate. But the curtain was pulled across the middle of the room, so I did not bother to see whoever it was.

Compared with the other room, I was somewhat more relaxed and very calm. Something was different. The energy was pure and loving. I thought I was losing it since I was woken up during my sleep because how could a hospital room feel so loving and warm?

As I colored a picture, I heard motion from the other side of the curtain. I looked down at the floor and saw a person walking toward the curtain to peek at me. At first glance, I thought it was my mom. I was ready to jump and give her the biggest hug. Her hair, body figure, and body movements were identical to my mother's. But it wasn't.

"Honey, where are your parents?" she asked.

"Oh hi! My parents are on a cruise for my brother's spring break," I answered.

"Oh no, do you need anything? Can I ask why you are here?"

I giggled because I didn't know where to begin, so I invited her to sit at the end of my bed as I told her my story. As I was explaining, a huge weight was lifted off her shoulders and tears started flowing from her eyes.

"You are the angel we have been praying for! Oh my gosh, this is a miracle," she exclaimed.

To say the least, I was stunned and actually freaked out. I wanted to scream to my nurse to make me move rooms.

"I thank you, but why am I the answer to your prayers? And who is we? And who are you exactly?" I asked.

I turned to see the curtain getting pushed back, and I made eye contact with a female who looked my age standing there, fragile and desperate for her mom to help her make her way to the bathroom.

I then watched the scene of this poor girl who had no strength to walk to the bathroom. She seemed so sweet, gentle, and innocent, and I thought, why was God making her suffer like that? As she was in the bathroom, I continued to color with thoughts running through my head.

The bathroom door swung open, and she quickly made her way out and said, "You were born with TEF? You had a feeding tube when you were little? And you are here now because you cannot vomit? And you didn't die?" she exclaimed like she found her light.

All I could do was smile, but I was cautious as to how I presented myself as a miracle baby born with TEF.

She came up close to me and said, "Finally! I am not alone. You are my angel."

I was still confused as to why I was the "angel." After she had her praise-Jesus moment, I asked her why she was in the hospital. She told me how she was just twenty-three years old and one day started getting sick. Her body could not stop vomiting, and she had to get a feeding tube put in. She was diagnosed with an autoimmune chronic illness and was experiencing all the same symptoms that I do.

I wish I could say I controlled that whole situation, but I didn't. What we all witnessed in that hospital room was the beautiful gift from God called divine grace. I showed her my scars, and we exchanged stories and similarities. The energy was loving and full of light. To this day, I believe that was the Divine's way of showing me who really is in charge and how we all have the ability to be someone's angel. Not going to lie, I felt like I was seeing my twin. We had similar names, our parents had the same types of jobs, and we both had a brother for a sibling. It was in our soul contract to meet. Once we spent several hours talking, my nurse came in and said it was time for me to go. I got to be released.

Happy? Yes. But then I felt like I was just getting to share and to connect with someone on a level that not many people can relate with me on. So as I was packing up my belongings, I noticed her get-well section was a little dim, so I gave her a balloon and wrote "Shine bright!" on it. It was since that moment when I learned that no matter how hard or challenging life can be, there is always a reason for it, and it is up to us to make sure we shine bright.

Weeks went by and she and I kept in touch. I was that ear she needed during her time of need. She is now happily married but still living with chronic illness. She now helps people by writing on her blog and sharing her story.

After my week at the hospital, my family finally arrived back on US soil. My parents learned about the situation and rushed home. Once I saw my mom, I started crying. She wrapped her arms around me and said, "It is okay. We are here now."

She said that because we all knew that this season of my journey was not over. That week in the hospital was just more of an episode. The rest of the summer, I was a grandma. Ironically enough, I was living in my apartment near school for the summer. Balancing the life of having an old body that works like a grandma and being a college student was eventful, to say the least.

The amount of diets they put me on was insane. The furthest I could walk was to our mailbox, which was right outside our apartment. I probably looked like a crazy person just walking the rate of a turtle in a college apartment complex. Since the diets weren't helping and the tests weren't showing enough information, I had to get a colonoscopy. Literally, a pain in the ass. What twenty-year-old gets a procedure done that people get in their fifties? Me—the answer is me.

I don't think my doctors realized how the liquids I had to drink the night before my procedure actually made me want to puke. Newsflash, people, I can't even get sick, so that evening was not one of my finest.

The sun was rising, and it was time to get a tube stuck up my butt! Woohoo! First time for everything. After the surgery, they still did not know what to do because they couldn't find a source that would explain my body's behavior.

A week later, they drew blood. My friend who experienced my hospital episode asked me if I wanted to go swimming, so we hung out at the pool all day long, nervous to put my swimsuit on because I felt like a pregnant elephant. It was until I got a phone call that shared the breaking news with me.

I was diagnosed with celiac disease, which meant all the bagels, pizza, pasta, sandwiches, desserts, and beer I was savoring had to stop. I hung up the phone and started laughing. I thought I was invincible until I met with my nutritionist who explained to me the seriousness of the disease and how I needed to act on it immediately.

Talk about sticking out even more in society. Everywhere I went with my friends or family out to eat, I had to be the special one and ask for a gluten-free menu. For a while, I got bombarded with so many questions like "Jess, want some pizza?" "Jess, what kind of beer do you want?" "Want some dessert my mom made?" friends would say.

My absolute favorite question goes to two of my high school best friends. We were out at Applebee's catching up, and I explained celiac and gluten for probably fifteen minutes. Once I was done, they looked like deer in headlights and said, "So gluten is sugar . . ." I busted out into laughter because they weren't kidding. They then offered some of their noodles and sandwich to me, not realizing I could not have both of those things.

A positive to this whole experience was that it taught me a lesson, which I will share with you, and that is this: Your body is your safe haven. It is your machine. Love it and take care of it. Yes, you can be human and eat poorly every now and then, but love your body because it makes you who you are. It surprised me on how much better I felt after I stopped putting gluten in my body. I was energized, excited, and finally back on my feet. The bloated feeling was gone, and I started to gain so much love for my body. I could go to dance practice and not rush to the bathroom and have an episode. I was able to enjoy more than four hours in the day compared to always sleeping and feeling drained.

When my mom and I went to the doctor for my follow-up, I was curious as to how I received celiac disease. My doctor said because of my history, my body is sensitive, which is not a bad thing. Then he asked me if I have ever gone through a stressful time in the past two years. I thought about it, and it clicked. My MIP experience was the most traumatizing and stressful time up to this point in my life. He explained the factors of what stress could do to your body overtime. Stress goes hand and hand with celiac disease. He told me to listen to my body and do something positive to it every day.

I really let the lesson sink in, and I made a promise with myself, and that was to discover a place of comfort that I could experience daily. Whether it was moving my body as I was listening to music, stretching before I went to bed, or going for a nature walk, I did it. One afternoon it was beautiful out, so I decided to go for a walk with no destination in mind. I told my roommate, "I would be gone for a couple of hours, so don't freak out." She just laughed and said, "Okay, Jess. Have fun exploring." Then I went. No phone, no music. Just me and Mother Earth. The amount of healing I received from this simple task was soul-moving. Friends would joke about the idea that they would know if I took a walk or not that day depending on my mood. They would say, "I think I saw you walking today." And most of the time, they were right. Little did I know I was paving my foundation and opening the door that would take me to the chapter of my journey where I learned we all have the power to heal ourselves. And when we do that, we heal this uncertain world.

I want you to make today the day where you start loving yourself. Write down statements that provide your body, heart, and soul love.

Go for a walk without your phone, go play golf, go find a beach, walk through the woods, and discover what your body is telling you. Today is the day to stop posting selfies and to take care and love yourself without caring how many likes you may get from the outside world. What are you waiting for? Make a move and go. The universe is waiting.

Exposing the Wound

In the society we live in today, having an internship in college is essential. It may be your door into the real world. For my degree, I actually needed to complete two internships, and they had to be from two different companies. The first internship I landed was for a semester at a local news station. This station was well-known across the lower part of Michigan, so it was a big deal. My supervisor was one of a kind. She was smart, creative, and motivating. She pushed our group to our highest potential. She paired us up with a reporter, writer, or producer. I was blessed to be paired up with one of the best producers around, well at least in my opinion. She didn't baby me. She pushed me and raised the bar high. Over the summer, we got to know each other pretty well. I would always leave the station with a lesson or piece of advice she provided me during our shift. When I apply for new jobs or start a new activity, I am always cautious on what I say about my health and my journey. People always say I am wise or I am an old soul, and I just nod and agree. I wait for the right time to actually open that door and share why I am the way I am. One morning I woke up and my body was not doing so well. I never know if it is going to be an all-day episode or just a morning one. I waited the morning out, and I knew I couldn't go to work. The next day I set up a meeting with my supervisor to tell her my story.

On my way to the station, I drove in silence as my heart was out of my chest, desperately holding on to the hope that everything would turn out okay. The door was shut, and she sat at her desk while I opened up to her. I did not know if I could get fired for not sharing this part of my life before I applied or if I would be suspended. After I was done, she looked at me and said, "Jessica, when I saw your application, I saw light. A bright light that got my attention. I felt that if we didn't hire you, it would have been the biggest mistake we would have ever made."

Just then, my view on my journey became light. I felt honored and worthy. I began to start tearing up because I never felt so relieved in my life. She then put her hands together on her desk, leaned forward, and said, "Now let me tell you my story."

She was diagnosed with lupus, which is a severe chronic stomach illness. I felt so connected to her it was scary. She told me her story so I could understand that I was not alone. We agreed it would be best to also tell the producer I was working with just so she was aware. The moment I shared with my supervisor was just one step closer to achieving my assignment I was given on this earth.

It was near the end of the summer, and energy started to change. I was finally on solid ground from my hospital episode and ready for the new school year. I knew, in the fall, my mom would have to have her first brain surgery, but I did not want to dwell on that thought just yet. My producer set up a special meeting with me, and I was unsure as to why. We walked into the conference room together, and she told me that if I wanted to for my final project, I could create my own news piece of my journey. Instantly, I felt the same feeling I had when my dance teacher told me I had to tell my story through dance. I took a deep breath and asked her to repeat herself. She told me it was time to share my story. We set deadlines for as to when the script, storyboard, filming, and editing all had to be done by. All responsibility was on me. As I left that day, I thought I was going to lose it. I love creating films and editing, but that is because I am sharing other people's stories—not mine. After a lot of hesitation, I finally got my big girl pants on and started brainstorming.

The whole process took about a month to complete. I interviewed my friend who was with me at the hospital, a dear friend from dance team, my wonderful roommate, and my parents. I also reached out to my main doctor at the children's hospital. By this time, it was a while since I have seen him or even walked the halls of the children's hospital. We set up a meeting to film an interview. Walking through the circle doors, noticing a playset to my left and right and the gift shop in the corner, I knew nothing had changed. I stepped onto the elevator, and to my surprise, my finger automatically pressed the right floor button. Of course, I was alone in the elevator, so I began talking to myself. The doors opened, and the flashbacks started happening just by seeing the waiting room. I kept my heart open, knowing that the flashbacks were okay and normal. I then made my way to the front desk, and they guided me to my doctor's office. Not going to lie, I started to tear up when I saw him for the first time in years. I was so little when he helped save my life, and to be able to thank him was such a moving experience. We sat down and started chatting. We filmed, and it went as smooth as it could. After that, I ventured through the halls, just soaking up the moment and allowing gratitude and strength in.

My roommate at the time helped me film it, and boy did we have a blast. I couldn't stop laughing about how many times I would mess up my lines. Her major is journalism, so needless to say, she saved the day on many occasions. She served as the angel that brought comfort and support throughout the entire process.

It was time to show my producer what I had created. Hesitant, yes, but ready to see what she would have to say. It was about six minutes long, and halfway through, she started crying. It was then when I realized how this video has the light and power to touch so many people. Once the video was over, she made some small technical critiques. She was blown away. I was pretty proud of myself too. She asked me if I was open to the idea of sharing it on their website. I am pretty sure the half of the lung I have stopped working. Their website is known all over the lower part of the state, which means my story would be shared with thousands. I got chills everywhere. I knew it was time to share it. On my last day, I got to witness a film I created on my own computer transferred on the station's main computer and then witnessed the timer go from 10 to 1. Boom—just like that, my story was out.

The amount of feedback I received from the video was unbelievable. E-mails and inboxes from people who suffer from chronic illness and were somewhat moved by my story. It was a feeling of strength, but more importantly, I learned how important and essential it is to open up your scars to the world because they bring light to others. Everyone you meet is facing a struggle or a battle. Be that light to someone. Smile at a stranger, buy someone's coffee, and volunteer somewhere. It is the little things in life that are most important. We all say it, post quotes about how to make the world a better place, but the question I have is this: What are doing about it? What actions have you taken to share your gift that you were blessed with? Your story has a special purpose and a unique light to it; let it shine because it will help others shine theirs. We are all in this together, so the time is to start right now and move together. Plus, when you share your story, you somehow, in an angelic, Godly way, get healed too, so why not share your light?

For the first time in years, I felt on top of the world. It was time to start my junior year of college. I was ready to face whatever life was going to throw at me. I put my mom's health in a positive spot in my mind, put my MIP experience behind me, and dedicated my life to live in a way of purpose and healing. Since my roommate at the time was an athlete, she had to live on campus during the school year, which meant I needed to find some new roommates. Living with people is an experience in itself. You learn what type of person you are by the little things. For instance, are you the one who takes out the garbage and puts a new roll of toilet paper when it is finished? Or are you the one who waits for the other person to take care of it? Or are you mixture of both? By this chapter of my life, I have lived with five different people. I am thankful for my experience with all of them because they continued to teach me lessons; however, it was not easy. Even though there were hard and frustrating days with them, they were an important part in my journey, and I thank them for treating me the way they did.

I ended up having a little whisper and feeling that I should call a dear friend of mine that I have known my entire life. She ironically has been connected somehow, someway, to many moments of my life. We played soccer with each other when we were just five years old, and a beautiful friendship began. We experienced the ups and downs high school brings with each other. We sat in the back in chemistry and did absolutely nothing because we were so lost, so we just passed notes to each other.

She was such a loving soul that everyone loved her. She recently just got back from studying abroad over in Europe. Thought she was crazy, but hey, why not! She had a party before she left, and once again, I had this strong sensation I had to go. She came back even more adventurous and brighter than she did before. As her friend, I was just so happy to see her happy all the time. She loved her family, was dating a new guy whom she loved very much, and she just traveled across the world! When I called her to see if she wanted to live with me, that same afternoon, she came over, walked through the apartment, and said, "Jess, I am moving in." A couple of weeks later, her family helped her unpack, and a new season was about to begin!

I reached out to another potential roommate who was on the dance team with me. I am very energy-sensitive, and I always listen to what my body tells me when I am around individuals. When all three of us were together for the first time, I knew my prayers were answered. I was blessed with two best roommates I could have ever asked for. The first night we all lived together was one for the books. We danced, drank, took pictures, chatted, and made our mark on Apartment 1004 together. We made it our home—a place I was always eager and excited to go to.

Divine Storm

There was something special about the connection Macy, Amber, and I had while we lived together. I always looked forward to coming home because no matter what kind of day I was having, they would make it ten times better. They served as the sisters I never had. They learned very quickly on how I am easily frightened, so they would gang up on me and jump out at me or surprise me with little things, like coloring my eggs in the fridge. We did a lot together, and every time we were together, we were on top of the world.

One day we decided to paint the apartment because it needed a facelift. At the time, Amber's family was building a new house, so she had some leftover paint. I painted the living room, Amber painted the kitchen, and Macy painted the entryway. We thought Macy was going to paint just around the door, but she decided to paint all three walls a bright color yellow. Somehow she got paint on the ceiling, but we just let it be. We asked her why the color yellow and why paint all three walls, and she said, "I want to enter this apartment happy, and I want to leave this apartment happy, and the color yellow allows me to do that." Amber and I agreed that she did have a point, so we let her finish her beautiful masterpiece without any thought about how deep that statement would become.

Halloween was right around the corner, which meant it was time to have a blast and find some fun costumes. A couple of weeks before, Macy and I agreed we would go to the store together to go shopping for costumes. She and her boyfriend were going to do a "themed costume," and I wasn't sure what I was going to be. Back in high school, we went Halloween shopping together; so we thought, why not continue the tradition?

One night Macy came home smiling ear to ear. She said she wanted to make dinner for Amber and me. Now we each had a unique role in the apartment. Amber was the cook, Macy was the go-getter, and I was the mom. Macy and I lacked cooking skills. In fact, one time we almost burned the apartment down! The alarm was going off, and we had no idea what to do. I asked, "Why make us dinner?" and she responded and said, "Because you guys deserve it! And I made sure it is all gluten-free." I felt so loved. No one has ever made me dinner unannounced like that. I offered to help, but she insisted that I keep sipping my wine and enjoy the evening. The following night, she did the same thing. She was all dressed up. She was wearing a white lace fall shirt with jeans and boots. I could tell she used my wand for her hair, and she was wearing a little bit of makeup. I asked why she looked so nice, and she said, "I am not sure. I just felt like getting ready."

The next day was Tuesday, October 22, 2013, Amber and I got back from dance team practice and Macy was in the shower. Amber looked at me as I was cleaning the dishes and said, "Jess, I feel like all three of us need to celebrate our friendship. Let's go get food." I agreed, and plus, who doesn't love food? So I ran into the room Macy and I shared and knocked on the bathroom door and said, "Macy, we are going to get food. Hurry up!" Within forty-five seconds, she was dressed and ready to go.

We ventured to Applebee's where we laughed and talked for hours. The strengths of our friendships were explained and how it is such a blessing that God brought all of us together. We talked about the concerts we went to, the adventures to Walmart at three in the morning, the amount of Nutella we would eat, the McDonald's trips, the cider mill, and the jokes about how Macy and I would most likely one day burn down the apartment because of our amazing kitchen skills. We talked about what to expect for our twenty-first birthdays since Macy's birthday was two days after mine. We planned on getting Amber a fake ID, so she could experience the good times. We discussed our weddings and how we were going to be one another's bridesmaids. But most importantly, we all agreed on how beautiful and amazing life was and how we were so happy with what God had given us and had such high hopes for the future.

It was getting late, so we decided it was time to go back to the apartment and get some sleep. Macy and I said good night to Amber as she went into her room and went to bed. Macy and I walked into our room and started our nighttime routine. She would plan out her outfit for the next day, and I would brush my teeth in the bathroom, and then we would switch. But this night was different.

We were getting ready, and an angelic energy was present, and I knew she felt it too.

I looked at her and said, "I know this is out of the blue, but do you believe in heaven?"

Her blue eyes lit up, and for the next hour, we discussed everything the Book of Life has to offer.

We talked about what would happen if one of us died before the other, what we would do and what we would want our friends and family to know. She told me she would look out for my little brother, and I told her I would put her little sister under my wing. We agreed we would stand as the shoulder to lean on when the families grieved. We agreed that even though the body dies, your soul still lives on. It journeys to a new beginning with the angels and the Divine, that when the body dies, it is time to celebrate the soul and the journey it made on this world.

I told her if I went to heaven before she did, that I would like a specific song to be played at my celebration. We then sat and listened to the song "I Lived" by One Republic. Once the song was over, we looked at each other and both knew we were crazy for having such a deep conversation, but we accepted the promise we made. We turned off the lights, said good night, and rested our heads on our pillows with no worries about what the next day would bring.

The Day the World Turned Upside Down

Beep Beep Beep!

The sounds of Macy's alarm clock forced me to jump out of bed with my heart out of my body. I ran over to her side of the room and tried to turn it off. It was so loud, and it was at five o'clock in the morning, so I was not a happy camper. I was so confused because Macy worked the 4:00 a.m. shift, so why on earth would she set an alarm for five o'clock? But I was too tired to think, so I ran back to bed with plans on going back to sleep. Well, that didn't work so much. Thoughts kept coming to my mind, and it was unsettling. It was finally time for me to get up. I got my clothes on, brushed my teeth, and set goals for the day. I heard Amber in her room, so I ran to say good morning. As she was brushing her teeth, I brought up the fact that Macy's alarm woke me up at five o'clock and asked if she knew why Macy would set an alarm at that time. Amber was still sleepy, so she just looked at me and said, "Jess, don't worry. It is fine. I am making bacon."

All day I tried to let it go, and around noon is when I started to feel sick. It almost felt like something was happening outside of my control. I knew I was in great Jessica health, I didn't eat any gluten, but I still felt like something was wrong. All day, I had that feeling. I went to class, didn't find the source; worked out, didn't find the source.

As soon as I pulled up to the apartment, the achy feeling got stronger. At this point, all I thought about was lying down before I had to teach. Ironically enough, it was a beautiful fall day. Sun was shining, weather was cool, leaves were changing—totally Instagram-worthy. As I opened up the apartment door, a gush of eerie energy came over me. The apartment was dark and quiet. It was not the apartment that was welcoming, warm, and cozy. The energy I felt was dark and mysterious—totally made the feeling worse. I went to the bedroom, and I felt as if I was being guided or tugged at the wall with pictures on it. As I looked at the pictures, a yellow light was shining from a picture of Macy and me on our senior spring break. I then got happy. I thought to myself on how blessed we were to be in each other's lives, especially after the conversation we had the night before. Moments like her making me gluten-free dinners two nights in a row, being able to say whatever we wanted, and going to Walmart at three in the morning all played in my mind. I then planned on buying her ice cream later that day just to show her how much I loved her.

My face was then guided to look at her bed. I felt really odd just staring at her bed, but then I ended up making her bed. Then I was freaked out, and so I ran into the kitchen, and I still felt this ache. I got my stuff and booked it out of the apartment. Now I will admit I believe I am a pretty good driver. However, the amount of times I checked my rearview mirror on my way to work was absolutely insane.

I pulled up to the studio and was two hours early. I urged for the music to make the ache go away, but it just stuck. My little ballerinas entered the door, and I mentally focused on having a good class. I looked at my phone and had a missed call from a 248 number and a voicemail. I thought that was weird but was not surprised because of the day I was having. I usually teach for at least three hours a night, but this night I had a mandatory school event to attend. I told my sub what the agenda was and how much I appreciated her coming in. She could tell I was acting strange, but she just let me be.

I ran out of the studio to make sure I would get to class on time. I listened to the voicemail, and it was Macy's boyfriend, curious to see if I had any idea on where she was. First thing I did was call Macy and was going to say I am not playing peacemaker today. Thought it was strange that she did not answer. Macy and her sister are best friends, so I thought, *Hey, maybe she knows where Macy is*, so I called her. No answer.

I did not want to, but I called Macy's boyfriend back to tell him I did not know where she was, but I had to go to class, so I could not help. After a couple of rings, he finally answered. My goal jumped out the window as soon as he picked up the phone. I heard tears, emptiness, and silence—similar to the sound of brokenness when I got the phone call about my mother's brain tumor. He was speechless and was unable to catch his breath. I kept asking if he was okay and what was going on.

He finally caught his breath and asked, "Have you spoken to Macy's family?"

"No, I have been teaching, and I am on my way to turn papers in. What is going on?" I demanded.

"I don't"—tears—"want to tell you." More tears. "I can't . . . tell you . . ." He paused.

I was getting frustrated, and I demanded to be told what the hell was going on.

He responded and said, "There was an accident. Macy is dead."

Boom—the achy feeling vanished, and I became raw. I was no longer dancing on solid ground. I was in the middle of hell. I hung up the phone because Macy's younger sister was calling me back. I did not even give her time to talk, and I just asked her if it is true, and she said yes. She told me they were at the hospital.

While I was still driving, I somehow got the strength to call my mom. I called her about ten times and no answer.

"Now is not the time to not answer your phone, Helene!" I screamed as if she could hear me.

I was losing strength and vision of the road because gallons of water were covering my eyes; I pulled off the highway into a strip mall. I sat in my car with it still running just frozen—completely frozen.

My body jumped when I heard my ringtone, and it was my mom.

"Mom, Mom, Mom . . . Macy is . . . Ma . . . cy is . . . Macy is dead."

She yelled at me to calm down because she had no idea what I was saying. She finally put it together and figured it out. She demanded me to stay exactly where I was and she would come get me, to turn my car off, and to not move.

My chin lay against my chest, and my shoulders caved in. My phone rang again, and it was my I-believe-I-can-fly friend who also was close to Macy. All she asked was if it was true. I used all the strength I could to respond to her with the truth because I knew I was going to be the person sharing the news of the tragedy. All I could think about was Amber and how I had to tell her, how she just met Macy and they became so close so fast, how much Amber looked up to Macy and how I was going to shatter Amber's world. I asked Amber to tell me where she was and if she was with someone. I told her to sit down and that I was so sorry, there has been an accident and Macy is dead. After I hung up the phone, everything died inside of me because our sisterly pack was broken. *Our lives will never be the same again*, I thought.

Ten minutes later, the wave of darkness washed over me.

He sprinted toward me as I collapsed. My eyes refocused to stare at the sky, looking up and asking why. Everything I believed in backstabbed me, leaving me fragile and not knowing how to take a single step forward.

His hands wrapped around my waist to catch me as I crumbled down. My arms draped over his shoulders, and he held me tight so I would not let go.

Sweat and tears dripped off my forehead as I sobbed. Catching my breath felt impossible since I was drowning in emotions, weeping and hollering as he was taking my parka off since I was on the verge of passing out, blinking my eyes to wake up from the nightmare, pushing my hands through my hair to release the pressure from my head.

"It can't be true." My hands made contact with my pale damp face. "It just can't."

My godfather was the first person to witness my grief.

Every part of my life, I have had to fight for. The world I believed that was filled with love, beauty, and happiness suddenly turned into an eerie, dark, foggy place in just one moment. It's a place where I no longer wanted to shine.

My godfather is my mom's brother. My mom called him because he lived right by the strip mall I was at to tell him what happened and how I was alone and emotionally unstable.

Once my mother found us, she said she talked to Macy's mom and that we were allowed to go to the hospital. My mom hopped in the backseat with me, and my godfather drove us to the hospital.

When Macy was getting transported from the accident to the hospital, they found brain activity, so they completed an emergency surgery on her. Every part of her body was fine except her brain. During surgery, they took some of her brain out because it was so swollen.

She survived surgery, so she was put on life support.

The car ride to the hospital was a blur. I just remember looking out the window and sobbing with my mom rubbing my back and my uncle driving.

He pulled up, and I do not even think I said goodbye or even thank you. I just started sprinting through the hospital sliding doors and running down the never-ending maze of hallways with no care of waiting for my mom, desperately searching for an answer. Finally, in the distance, I saw a familiar face. Macy's sister turned around, and we made eye contact.

Her head rested heavily on my shoulders as the rest of her body collapsed as she wept. My mom caught up with us and guided us to the service desk.

"Who are you here to visit?" the receptionist asked with a concerned look.

After a couple of seconds of silence, my mom spoke. "Uhh, Ma . . . cy."

I could not get enough courage to say her name, let alone get over the fact that I was currently standing in a hospital to see my roommate and lifelong friend on her deathbed.

Her shoulders caved in, and she looked down as if like she knew something we didn't know.

"She is in ICU, so you will need a special pass. I am sending healing thoughts. I am so sorry for your pain. We are hoping for a miracle."

Once we got our pass, we ran.

As we got in the elevator, I started to laugh. I guess that is what shock does to you. Once I started laughing, so did my mom and Macy's sister. For that half a minute, I felt joy. The elevator doors opened, and I stepped onto the ICU floor where joy was nowhere to be found.

As time passed, more and more people came to the hospital to support the family. Amber and I stood by each other the entire time, crying on each other's shoulder, holding hands, being each other's support system. The doctors told us that the goal is for Macy to make it through the night, but it would be a miracle if she did. Macy's family wanted to be alone, so we all left. My mom drove Macy's boyfriend and I home, and all we talked about was how happy Macy was, how she loved life, and how this had to be a nightmare. This was not happening.

That night was the night I became the messenger. By this time, the whole city of Troy was blowing up my phone, searching for answers, for which I do not blame them. I remember I slept in my parents' room because my dad was working out of town and my brother was at school, so there was no way I would go back to the apartment and sleep by myself. I did not want to sleep because that meant when I would wake up the next morning, the nightmare would be true. Facing reality sucks.

Over the next five days, that hospital was everyone's home. Country music was played, pictures were hung, and her favorite sheep on a stick lay next to her. Food, drinks, and flowers took over the ICU. The ICU was located on the top floor of the hospital, so when you looked out, all you saw where trees and the sky, kind of relaxing in some ways.

I remember the first time walking into the hospital room where she lay with bandages on her head felt as if I was walking on eggshells. I did not know where to turn or where to look. She lay there as the life support machine controlled her breathing, white leg braces wrapped around her shins so she did not get any blood clots, and her skin glowing as if nothing ever even happened. I stood there and wept as "My Wish" by Rascal Flatts played on the radio. My soul felt that she was telling me something, but my human instinct denied it. I did not say a word to her while I was in there. I prayed that she was happy and comfortable, even if that meant she had to go.

It was Friday morning when only her family, boyfriend, and I were there. We got news that it was not looking so good. I remember running out to the lobby and looking out the window as tears flowed down my face, breaking in ways I didn't even think were humanly possible. Her boyfriend was sitting down in the chair with his head in his hands crying. We just looked at each other and stayed silent. Her dad came out and said, "We are not giving up. We cannot give up. That is my girl, and we are not giving up."

We shook it off and bravely stepped into the next step of the journey.

Friday was the day that Macy and I were going to get our costumes and then have a roomie night and pick out pumpkins. After we got the news it was not looking good, I had a whisper that morning to have everyone over and carve pumpkins. Confused, but I went with it. Surprisingly enough, all our high school friends came home that day. It was emotional and bittersweet to see all of them, especially our friend who is in the Coast Guard. Seeing him just made my heart break because I had to face the reality that this was actually happening. We all met at my house and drove to a farmer's market. The old guy asked us what we were all doing carving pumpkins since it was a huge group. We told him the story, and we ended up getting our pumpkins for half off and the smaller ones for free! We carved our pumpkins and spelled out "We love you, Macy." The picture ended up on the front page of the newspaper the next morning.

Friday night, the city of Troy held a candle vigil at our high school. Hundreds of people showed up where we placed the pumpkins and candles and gathered together to pray for Macy and the family. I remember the band played a song; the news showed up, and people keep asking me questions because everyone relied on me. To be honest, that's all I remember.

Sunday night, the nurses gave Macy a spa day—painted her nails and did her hair. They were getting her ready for surgery the next day since some of the swelling went down and they could operate. Macy's family, boyfriend, a childhood friend, and I all surrounded our angel in her bed. I brought my little stuffed dog Lucky to be there for Macy. As I leaned forward and placed Lucky by her head, I had a whisper and feeling that I needed to say something positive. I reached out and touched her mom's shoulder and told everyone how no matter what happens, we will be okay. We will be there for one another, and we will get through this. Looking back on it, Macy was communicating through me and whispering in my ear because there was no way I said that all by myself.

We gave her a kiss on the head and left with high hopes for the next day. The sun was shining, and the air was calm. As soon as we got in the car, David Nail's "Whatever She's Got" came on the radio. Weeks before the accident, Amber, Macy, her sister, and I stood front row at David Nail's concert just to go for that song. We knew every time we heard David Nail or Luke Bryan, it was her doing.

Some nights I wanted to be by campus since I was still attending class. I stayed at my friend's apartment, the same friend who was with me during my hospital episode. We were in the same friend group, and all our friends came over and watched movies eating ice cream. I did my best to "fit in" and just focus on the current moment, but it was challenging. My friends were sweethearts and gave me hugs as I went to bed.

Before I closed my eyes, I wrote Macy a note that I hoped to read to her the next day before her surgery. Once the note was finished, I closed my eyes and went to bed. For the first time since the accident, I woke up refreshed. I went to class and actually paid attention until I received a text asking why the hospital was not allowing anyone to visit her today.

I responded back white lying, explaining that she was getting surgery, so maybe they did not want any visitors and did not think twice about it. After class, I gathered my belongings, ventured campus, and was extremely grateful for the day and the sun. I remember walking into the Oakland Center and seeing a bunch of my friends and teammates eating lunch, so I sat down with them. Through this whole process, I never really was hungry, but my summer roommate offered to get me a Snickers ice cream bar, so I thought, *Hey, why not eat some ice cream?* As she went to go get my ice cream, I got up and walked around the cafeteria to see if anything would jump out at me, but nothing did.

When I got back to the table, I noticed I had a missed call from the boyfriend of Macy's sister, who ironically is my brother's best friend. The image I remember is the Snickers ice cream bar sitting right next to my phone. I was hesitant to call him back, but I did anyway. Once he answered, I knew. Well, I obviously did not want to believe it, but I knew.

He said, "Jess, I . . . am . . . so . . . sorry."

I kept saying "No, no, no" over and over. Sweat and tears fell from my face. My journalism summer roommate friend grabbed me so I would not collapse. Everyone at the table was watching me in complete shock. Once I got off the phone, I ran to the hallway away from everyone. I remember shaking and seeing everything in black and white. I called my mom, and she was crying too because she found out. She told me that she would meet me at the hospital if I got a ride. I kept pacing back and forth in front of the bathrooms, not sure what to do.

I got myself together and knew I had to break the news to Amber once again. She answered the phone and just screamed, "No. How could she? No, Jess, no. She can't die. Jess, no!" I will never forget the way her voice sounded. The news broke her, and I was the one that gave her that news.

Somehow, someway, I walked back to the table still seeing black and white and felt nothing but stares. They did not want to believe it, so they were waiting for me to say it was not true until I explained I needed a ride to the hospital. By the time I opened up my mouth, everyone just broke. My summer roommate and my German friend got their stuff and told me they would take me. Everyone hugged me tight and told me they would pray for me and that they were so sorry. I remember walking with a purpose and running to my friend's car just in complete shock and almost laughing because I was so overwhelmed and I did not want to believe it was true.

We all got in the car, and country was playing. I started hollering because the pain was attacking me from all ends, and I felt nothing but emptiness and anger. I gave my keys to my other friend so she would drive my car to the hospital so my car would be there. Thank God for them. Once again, probably traumatized both of them throughout this whole process.

We arrived at the hospital, and I ran as fast as my little body could. I ran through the hospital doors and saw her mom and sister sitting on the couches in a traumatized daze. Their bodies had no soul to them. I mean, how could they?

I held on to them and did not let go. No one said a word. Just emptiness, sadness, and uncertainty. Moments like these, you do not need to speak. You already know what is being communicated.

They then told me what had happened. When the doctors checked her brain activity early in the morning, there was none. The next twelve hours served as a waiting period. Three doctors have to confirm no brain activity. By the time I got there, two doctors already confirmed it.

As time passed, the ICU lobby was filled with family, friends, neighbors, teammates, and loved ones. Before the last set of doctors went into her room, we all stood in a circle and prayed together. We gathered together, walked down the hall and into her room to say our final goodbyes. Everyone was sobbing and in an emotional daze. Even the nurses and doctors stood in silence and grief. After our goodbyes, we went into the lobby where we waited for the doctors to tell us what they found.

The heavy door unlocked, and soft slow heel steps make their way down the hallway. No one is talking, let alone breathing. We all held our breath; well, at least I know I was. A group of white coats came out into the lobby and pronounced the time of death and walked away. I was sitting in a chair up against the wall, and just like that, darkness. I felt as if I was drunk on a carousel trying to see straight. My mother came to me and held me tight. I wanted to hug her back, but I could not move. I stopped breathing because if I knew if I took a breath, I was not dreaming. After a couple of moments, I took my first breath, collapsed into my mother's arms, and wept. We were living in a nightmare.

Being the messenger is a bittersweet role. When there is positive news to share, that was always easy, but this? How do I even tell everyone that she died? She will never walk on this earth again. She would never come home to the apartment again, she won't have a wedding, and her family went from four people to three. The nightmare had happened, and there is no way to fix it. I took a deep breath, and just as I started the message, a gush of powerful energy came over me. Looking back at what I wrote, I knew it was not really me who wrote that. It was the angels and Macy who were communicating through me, bringing love and light to the message.

One of the hardest things to face was the apartment and to walk into the room that we shared. Now over the five days, I did eventually have to go back and pack some things. In fact, on one of the times I went back, I noticed one of Macy's picture frames on the wall was uneven. It looked like someone pushed it off the nail. Thought it was creepy, hilarious, and powerful all at the same time. But those moments were when I hoped she would make it.

Entering the apartment for the first time since she went to heaven was unbearable. I sat on my bed, staring at hers, knowing she would never sleep in it again. I walked into the closet knowing her clothes and shoes will never be worn again. I sat alone in the room we shared just in utter shock. Over the time when she was in the ICU, everyone discussed where she was going or driving to. We put the pieces together and figured out she was going to the Halloween store. The guilt I felt thinking about how we were supposed to go together still haunts me today. What if I was in that car? What would have happened? What if I got back to the apartment that day sooner to go with her? I knew she would not want me to think like that, but I am human, so I did. After throwing myself a pity party, I started packing up her belongings because the thought of having her mother do that was heart-wrenching. I put some country music on and took my time packing up her precious belongings. I found myself giggling and then crying some more. Every article of clothing she had brought back a memory. But then, just like that, gone. Her mom and a family friend came the next day to take the stuff home. The transition from having a place we called home to in one day turn into a place of hell was unsettling. It took months to make that apartment home again. I tried my best to fill up the empty space. To be honest, it never really hit that level of love and comfort it had before the accident happened. You can never replace a spirit so full of love and light.

During this time, I really did not know what to do. Some days I still do not know what to say or to feel. Do you cry in a dark room by yourself, or do you go along with your day like nothing ever happened? Who do you talk to about it? Are you allowed to say stuff like "I feel like I am dying"? When you go through something tragic, you ultimately are lost, not just emotionally but mentally and physically. You question everything. You question your own life, and you are on a constant search for answers. Sadly, those answers were never found in the ways we hoped them to be.

Macy went to heaven on Monday, October 28, 2013, five days after the accident. There is my answer about her alarm clock going off at five in the morning on October 23. The Divine was communicating to me on how I had five days left with Macy before she was with them up in the divine world. During this time, I also faced the reality of the connection of the color yellow every time I walked in and out of the apartment and the phrase "enter happy and leave happy" came into full effect. To top it all off, our last conversation we had was what would happen if one of us died. I cannot make this stuff up.

The night of her funeral, my high school friends and I went up to Michigan State and threw a party. Childish? Yes, but what else are we supposed to do? We were never handed a book in school that taught us the proper way to grieve when a friend dies at the age of twenty in a tragic car accident.

The next day was a basketball game that we had to dance at. They did a moment of silence before announcing the players in honor of Macy. I can't even tell you how Amber and I danced with smiles on our faces, but we did because we knew that is what Macy would want us to do.

Life has never been the same since that day. How could it? But the dark days were not over just yet.

ICU Round Two

Exactly three weeks after Macy died, I had to ask for another ICU pass to visit my mom in the hospital after her first brain surgery.

Because I was still raw from the accident, I was an energy magnet. As my dad and I were waiting in the ICU lobby during my mom's surgery, I overheard an older lady on the phone explaining the news and the progress about her husband who was also in the ICU. I wanted to know the whole story, so I observed who she was with, how they treated her, and really believed he would make it. My mother's doctors came out and said surgery went well even though I did not quite believe him. I did not know why I did not believe him. But I just did not believe him.

The nurses led us to the main doors where I was experiencing nothing but emotional triggers. Pressing a button to enter the ICU, not being able to have cellphones, being quiet as you walked through the halls, it was all too real too soon. I wanted to escape, but there was no way out. I had to stand strong for my mom because she just had brain surgery.

I observed the whole ICU floor. Each hospital room surrounded by glass doors and windows, which means you could see inside each room. I passed a room, and a patient was on his bed but hanging from the ceiling. I saw patients whose necks were twisted and turned in ways I did not even think was possible. I witnessed loved ones grasping on to the hospital beds and not wanting to let go. I was witnessing strangers' darkest days as well as realizing I unfortunately understood what those strangers were feeling.

Ironically enough, the way Macy was laid was the exact same way my mother was. Talk about an emotional trigger and traumatizing visual. However, my mother's face was swollen and black and blue. The area around her nose was yellow because the kind of surgery she had included tubes to be traveled through her nose to get up into the brain to remove her tumors.

I looked up at one of my mom's screens, and a red button started flashing, and five seconds later, a beeping noise started going off. I panicked because hospital sounds are not that pleasing to the ear, and I thought something was wrong with my mom and how I could not lose her. Out of nowhere, a stampede of machines was being pushed down the hallways and doctors screaming and running.

They ran into a room where a gentleman was lying. He must have been a teacher or something because his room was filled with pictures and notes from students. I watched from my mom's room in a frozen daze. Over twenty-five people were in the room, trying to bring the man back to life. Machines and cords everywhere, demands and commands were being stated. Felt as if I was in the middle of an episode out of *Grey's Anatomy*.

After a long time, the stampede turned silent. All hands were removed from the patient, and the time of death was announced. It was then when I looked at the ICU doors opening up and in walks the lady I was observing in the lobby. Her family surrounded her as she was sobbing, walking with fear in her eyes, knowing she was walking the path that will end up leading her to her dead husband. I had no idea what to do. I felt the pain and the grief. I felt as if I was watching myself in the reflection of a shattered mirror. *Was that how we all looked when we said our final goodbyes to Macy?* I thought.

I couldn't help but just stare. I looked like a deer in headlights. It was since that day I saw this world in black and white.

Turns out, my mom's surgery did not work. She got worse. The surgeon messed up and she can no longer smell and taste. Unfortunately, she most likely will not be able to get them back. She went into a deep depression. Imagine grieving and coming home and seeing your mom who is full of love and light sitting on the couch in the dark just staring or even finding her frozen on the floor or hearing her cry all day and every day.

It breaks my heart even sharing this with you, but it is the truth— the truth that mental illness and depression do exist in this world and have huge effects on everyone involved. It is our job as messengers to shine love and light to it and to bring awareness to it; to let them know they are not alone; to start nonprofits, organizations, or even clubs for individuals to provide a place of comfort and love to allow them to heal.

Laughing Angel

One quality I have is that I am stubborn, really stubborn, so accepting the fact that I was experiencing rock bottom was not pleasant. My thoughts were not healthy for my self-esteem and self-care. I belittled myself. I was angry with myself. I was pissed at this uncertain world. I felt as if I was living a double life, one that was dark and another that was light. People know me as the "shining bright warrior," so how could I show any weakness? I think I even made a positive Facebook post about my mom's recovery just so it would seem like I was fine.

On top of dealing with my unhealthy perspective of this uncertain world and having a mom whose illness was taking over, I needed to find another person to live with. Amber and I could not pay for it just us two. We both knew what we had to do, which was finding another roommate to take Macy's place, once again facing the heart-wrenching reality that this was really happening: Macy is gone.

Being the mom that I am, I found one. I subconsciously was desperate for control. I wanted to show the world that no matter what the odds were, I would stand tall. What was the problem with this? I was not allowing myself to feel my true emotions or even heal from them.

Looking back at it, I am not really sure how it happened, but one of my friends from high school moved in with Amber and me. He is the life of the party. He lived in the same subdivision growing up as Macy, so I didn't have to explain to him why we needed another roommate. He was feeling and living through the tragedy too.

He moved in around Thanksgiving, just a couple of weeks after the accident. During that time, Macy's belongings were out. The apartment was empty. Love and joy were no longer present. Amber and I did our best to work it out and be there for each other, but grief is one of the hardest life lessons to live with, especially when it is tragic.

Ever since the day he moved in, he taught me the importance of laughter. Yes, I was at rock bottom, but somehow, someway, he made me laugh even if it lasted two seconds. Overtime, he became my brother. He would listen to me cry, listen to me vent, tell me if an outfit was ugly, fix my hair, help me rearrange the furniture at two in the morning, listen to Disney music with me, hand me a bottle of wine without saying anything, drove to Chipotle with me, inhale helium, create together, go on adventures in the pouring rain, sing our hearts out at concerts, and he just held me tight when I needed it. He accepted me when I didn't accept myself. He was the angel that kept me together. He was sent by God to not only support me but also to stand next to me side by side in the hellhole I currently was in. I am not sure where I would be without him and his soul lesson he brought to my journey. I can randomly stop by at his house, and he can do the same for me, and it wouldn't be awkward. Our friendship is one of the most authentic friendships I have ever had. Keep on laughing, angel. Continue on shining your light because, trust me, it heals.

Accepting the Unexpected

There came a point in my grief where I decided enough was enough. I was in class when the thought of going on a trip with a bunch of strangers to volunteer popped into my head. I had no idea where the thought came from, but I made sure I would give it some time to make its mark on my brain. The thought got stronger and stronger over the next couple of days to the point that it's all I could think about. I realized it was time to put my big girl pants on and to act on it—to open my heart to whatever the thought would lead me to even though I was fearful of the unknown.

I researched trips and groups that Oakland University had since I hardly branched out because of being involved in athletics. A group called Alternative Spring Break ironically enough popped up many times during my research. Usually, spring break means party time and letting loose; however, I knew that I would not benefit from that. My soul needed something more. I needed to know I wasn't the only one who was suffering in this world. I was desperate to escape and get away from my mess with people who had no idea of what my journey entails, to sharpen the way I look at this world through pure love rather than hate and fear, to share laughter and support for those who needed it. Why? I needed the chance to do something for myself and to live again. I needed to move forward in my journey.

A group was scheduled to travel to Chicago and volunteer at a children's center in the suburbs for a week. *This was obviously meant for me*, I thought. I love Chicago, and I love kids, so it is a win-win. I was hesitant to apply because the amount of practices and games I would miss was not fair to the team, especially being captain and it being the end of the season. I was in my bedroom doing homework when I was guided to read an article that was written about Macy's study-abroad trip which ironically enough was posted on our school's website just two days before the accident.

One of the goals of the article was to reach out to those who were uncertain about studying overseas and traveling the world. Near the end of the article, a quote said by Macy jumped off the newspaper and made my heart spin. "Just go for it," I read. I started to tear up because I knew that was her unique way of telling me to go. I thought to myself, *Jess, when was the last time you did something you actually wanted to do?* I took my sign, placed it in my heart, and went for it.

Of course, typical me, I realized the trip was scheduled three weeks from that day, and I may have missed my opportunity to even go. All the fund-raisers and meetings, I missed. Rushing to apply, I finished the application and apologized for the late registry. To my surprise, I received an e-mail not even five minutes later from the supervisor of the trip. She said they had one more opening because someone just dropped moments before I applied. Coincidence? I think not. I met her the following day, paid the full amount, and booked the trip.

I shared the news with my laughing angel, and his way of telling me he was proud of me was to look up horror stories of people staying in hostels and felt the need to share them with me.

My parents were out of town on the day when I had to be dropped off at a bus station down in Detroit. I was pissed and overwhelmed because I had to figure it out by myself. I was going on a bus with seventeen people who I never met before. I was nervous and needed some sort of comfort. I gave my parents a deadline to see if they could work something out to take me, but it did not happen. Nervous to ask for help, I reached out to my friend who took me to the hospital. She said she did not mind, so she ended up taking me. I don't even know if we talked in the car because second thoughts about going took over my focus. The devil was playing games with me. I tried to play it cool, but she could probably tell my bluff. We pulled up to the station and sat in the car for about five minutes until I saw some college-looking individuals venture to a bus just near the street corner.

My friend looked at me and said, "They all look nice," saying as if she could feel my sense of fear.

"Yeah. They do look nice," I said with a giggle.

I gave her a hug, hid some gas money in her car as a thank you, grabbed my belongings, and walked to the bus.

Remaining calm as I observed the situation was a bit of a challenge. To make sure I was not getting on a bus going to California or some other place, I asked a stranger if the bus was going to Chicago. I was in the right place.

I put my suitcase with all the other suitcases and walked up the stairs and stood in the aisle way just staring at the seats.

I literally do not know a soul on this bus. Why did I think this was a good idea? Where do I even go from here?" I thought. I tried to remain cool though. You know, to look like I had my shit together.

I captured a spot near the middle, and both seats were open. I, acting like I have it all together, marked my seat and sat next to the window.

More and more people were loading the bus, and I was interested to see what human would sit next to me. A petite African American girl boarded the bus, and she seemed sweet. She placed her pillow and backpack on the seat next to me, and I asked her if she knew anyone on this trip. A weight was lifted off my shoulders when she said she did not know anyone either.

To calm my anxious thoughts, I pulled out my coloring book as well as Lucky. I asked the girl next to me if she wanted to join me. Her eyes looked at my little stuffed dog and the coloring book as if I was too old to color and have a stuffed animal.

"Uh, haha, no, thank you," she said, looking at her iPod.

"Oh okay. Just thought I'd ask," I replied.

"Great start, Jess. way to go!" my ego screamed at me.

"Do you know the song 'I'm the Man' by Aloe Black? I love that song," I said, trying again to redeem myself.

"Um, no," she said as she was confused as to why I was still talking.

I tried my best not to judge her, but I was offended, which I eventually told her a couple of days into the trip once we got to know each other better. We became bus and coloring buddies. Now every time she hears that song, she thinks of me and laughs. First impressions are always fun.

I could see the Chicago skyline in the distance. Happy jitters filled my body as I realized this was really happening. For the first time in a long time, I was going after and conquering my life. Our bus dropped us off about two miles from our hostel. It was February in Chicago, so needless to say my body was not even all the way off the bus and I was frozen. I knew the only way I would survive this trip was to be my own motivator. I closed my eyes and repeated my favorite line from *Finding Nemo*, "Just keep swimming, just keep swimming."

The hostel was near in sight, and oddly enough, I got choked up. I was probably sleep-deprived, mentally and emotionally exhausted, so we will just blame it on those things even though that was the first time I felt like I actually accomplished something. The hostel was a lot nicer than what I expected, especially after reading horror stories researched by my laughing angel.

Seven girls and I shared a room and one bathroom. Cozy, huh? We each had our own lockers and bed. That was pretty much it. Our room was in the basement, and I picked the bed nearest to the window just in case I needed to escape or there was a fire. When you are depressed, you think of the craziest situations because you feel entitled to say tragedy can happen; and I was not fully healed then, so I did anything in my power to be prepared for whatever came next even if I had to freeze at night because of all the cold winter air coming from the window.

The way the system works while staying in a hostel is that there is one big kitchen where you make your own meals as well as clean the dishes. Fridges and freezers are piled with produce with sticky notes claiming individual's food. Because we had a group of about eighteen and we were not the only people staying in the hostel, each night we worked in groups to either cook dinner or wash the dishes. I accepted the fact that not many people really understand the idea of what celiac is, so I willingly knew it was mandatory for me to venture to the grocery store with my supervisor and trip professor. To my surprise, I was not the only one who was allergic to gluten. On the way to Chicago, I could observe that there was something special about this one individual. She was intelligent beyond my knowledge, very well-spoken, but uncomfortably blunt. She did not pick up social queues, but that never seemed to bother her. We paired up in the lobby of the hostel and walked to the grocery store. I became fond of her spirit and energy. I knew she had some kind of intellectual disability, but to me, that was not important. What was important was that she faces adversity every single day wherever she goes but still strives to give back love and light to a world that views her as "abnormal." For instance, as we were picking out crackers, she stood in the middle of the aisle because that was where she felt comfortable enough, though she was blocking other busy rushing Chicago customers. They would look at her as if she was breaking a law, but she just stood there confidently. The eyes then glanced over to me as if I was her caregiver or babysitter, but most of the time, I just let her do what she wanted because I was intrigued by her. The more I got to know her; I got to understand her way of thinking. She likes order, purpose, and action. She likes facts and works hard to get them if they are not present. I learned that she has a list of medical illnesses similar to me. That moment was when I realized my perspective of this unknown world was shifting.

To my surprise, the center we volunteered at was not just a place filled with little, adorable, loving kids. It was the place where kids who were put into foster care go but could not manage to sustain healthy relationships with families because of many sorts of influences, such as violence, alcohol, drug, sexual and physical abuse, divorce, rape, murders, etc. We walked in, and I could tell that we all were in for some culture shock. The director of the center welcomed us to a conference room where we got the lowdown of what happens in the center.

"These kids are just like any other kids in the world! However, know you are in for a week of uncertainty," he exclaimed.

The age of the children ranged from five years old to seniors in high school. Come to find out, it was not just an after-school program like I thought. The center was their home, where they eat, go to school, and sleep. I was sitting in a mental and emotional institution for children.

Overwhelmed with the thought of what these kids go through was enough for me to feel my heart break.

"Please understand that one day a child may be happy, and the next second they may be violent. These kids are sensitive. Be a role model because they do not have any. What we do here and what they learn here will determine their future, and we strive for bright futures in every one of our students," he said.

Violent! I thought. Oh, dear Lord in heaven, this is nothing like what I was expecting. As I glanced around the room to see faces of my group members, I knew I was not the only one who was sitting on their seat in a funny position. The director gave us a tour of the center, and my heart broke even more.

A picture, which illustrated a crime scene, created by a little six-year-old hung to the wall near his dresser. He used art therapy as a way of expressing what happened to his family. The bedrooms had no doors. The answer as to why there were no doors was it was an opportunity for violence for the child to commit. Glass was never found, doors always locked behind you, sounds of alarms would always go off, holes in the walls were normal to witness, as well as rooms with gymnastic mats walls. If you saw a child alone, all hell would break loose.

I was helping a little African American boy with his homework. As we were working on it together, he kept bringing up the topic about guns. He was probably seven, and he knew everything about a gun. Not knowing what to do, I asked him to explain the picture he drew in art class since it was an interesting picture.

"Ms. Jessica, this is a picture of my brother. He is wearing a blue shirt because that is what color shirt he was wearing when he got shot. I have not seen him since the shooting, so I wanted to draw a nice picture of him," he said.

I closed my eyes and squeezed my hands together, trying so hard not to break in front of this little innocent boy. What captured my heart the most was that the little boy's tone of voice and his attitude toward his brother getting shot was as if he was just ordering food.

It was not a big deal to him because he was around shootings all the time before entering the center. This was his normal. This was how he viewed the world because that was what he had been exposed to.

I was emotionally raw for the rest of the day and evening. I was so angry with God and the universe for putting these innocent children through such traumatic events. Being an empath did not help the situation out either. The next day I made a goal to work with the little boy again since I felt connected to him. The volunteers and I gathered in the cafeteria to meet the children. A couple of moments went by and I did not see him, which concerned me. I then hear his innocent contagious laugh from a distance, we made eye contact, and his face lit up with joy.

"Ms. Jessica, Ms. Jessica! Look at what I got on my homework we did together! Come look," he said.

He got an A, which made him feel important, and he felt like he could actually accomplish something.

As we were working on math problems—which, by the way, I had no idea how to do, but I just let it be—I asked him what he wanted to be when he grows up. His pencil slowly dropped onto his homework assignment, and his eyes turned toward me as if I was asking a confusing question.

"No one, besides my teachers, have asked me what my dreams are. Ms. Jessica, you are cool," he said as he went back to accomplishing his homework.

In that moment, the lesson of believing in one another presented itself. To me, it was a simple question that I get asked all the time. For him, his perspective on the idea of believing in yourself became a new adventure I hope he explores. I have faith that one day he will become the lawyer, schoolteacher, or big brother he dreamed to be.

It was lunchtime, so it was time to switch volunteers and children. I was sitting in my chair in the cafeteria waiting for the other group just pondering my thoughts about how my perspective on life grew in more ways than one. A little brown-haired girl interrupted my thoughts and sat next to me.

"Hi. What is your name?" she asked.

"Why, hello. My name is Ms. Jessica," I responded.

"Cool. Want to be my friend?" she asked.

"Of course. I would love to be your friend."

Observing the fact that she was wearing purple pants, a purple shirt, and a purple headband, I had a feeling she liked the color purple.

"Is your favorite color purple?" I asked.

"yes! How did you know?" she exclaimed.

"Just guessed. But guess what, my favorite color is purple too," I said.

"No way! Really? We really are good friends. Ms. Jessica, you rock!" she said.

I thought to myself, if only the world viewed friendship in this way. Instead of basing our friendships off who likes or follows each other on social media, I just gained a friend over our favorite color. Life can be simple—it is just a matter of how you look at it.

The little girl never left my side for the rest of the day. I noticed that she did not have many friends at the center, which bothered me. She would try to talk to kids in her class or group, but no one gave her any time of day. We were eating with kids from her group, and three girls were ganging up on her. I observed the situation to see if I should step in or not, and the three girls kept teasing her. Before I could intervene, two workers came over and pulled my friend away and told her she needed to take her medicine to calm down. I was thinking, she did not do anything wrong. Yeah, she is outgoing, but you do not need to force medicine down this little girl's throat just because she was bothering the other girls, which, quite frankly, they were the ones that started the whole event in the first place.

She was gone for about ten minutes. She saw me and started running toward me but was demanded to stop running. All she wanted was a hug or someone to tell her it was going to be okay. When she sat down, the first thing she said was this: "Don't worry, Ms. Jessica. I am fine."

I felt as if I was looking at my younger self in the mirror because I am the queen in using the statement—"I'm fine." I got choked up and excused myself from the assembly. I searched for the nearest bathroom, so I could go into a stall and cry.

Obviously made sure no one else was in the bathroom by checking to see if I saw any feet, but the coast was clear.

I wept for a couple of minutes in the bathroom stall and allowed myself to feel again.

I got it together and sat back down, and the little girl was curious as to why I left.

"Don't worry, friend. I am fine," I said.

During the first year of my grief, I hung on to dates like it was my job. Mentally, I kept count on how many weeks, days, and months it had been since the accident. It was my way of trying to wrap my mind around the thought that it did happen and I was not dreaming. For the rest of my life, the numbers 5, 23, and 28 will always have an emotional meaning behind them. The irony of the trip was that we left Detroit on the February 23 and we came home on the February 28. Those five days each month served as my period week because I did, in fact, lose my period for months after the accident.

The group I volunteered with was one of a kind. We all blended well. Obviously, just like anywhere you go, you become closer to a specific few, but for the most part, we stood as one family.

Like I said before, no one had any idea on my journey, but at the same time, I knew nothing about them. The girl who took the bunk above me was an adventurer. She loved to explore and just had a pure energy about her. We went to Starbucks together with our little group, but she and I were connecting on a soul level. We talked about life, meaning, purpose, and volunteering. She explained how she was getting ready to study abroad in the summer. I got really excited because I was given the opportunity to share Macy's study-abroad experience through happiness and joy rather than in tears and grief. As she was explaining where she was going to go, I had a whisper to ask her what program she applied to.

"It is a program through Oakland, but the group you travel with are students who do not attend Oakland. They are from all over the world. It is called CIEE," she said.

Instant happiness.

"You know, my friend and roommate studied abroad through that program and absolutely loved it. She went to Europe, and it was the best trip of her life," I said.

She looked at me and smiled.

"Is her name Macy?" she asked.

Once again, the universe shocked me and gave me chills. She could tell that it took me by surprise. My first time ever talking about Macy to a group of strangers was absolutely perfect. Come to find out, the people I met were not strangers to my journey of growth. They were essential in my rebirth to become who I am supposed to be.

The girls that were with us overheard us talking about Macy. I felt as if I was dreaming because somehow, someway, they all knew of her or of the accident.

"Wait, Jess, you knew Macy?"

"Yes, why?"

She pulled me aside and told me what roads she takes to get to school. Odd right? Well, on the day of the accident, she felt a very strong sense of energy to not take her usual way home. An important piece of information to know about this girl is that she is not the best with directions, so this energy confused her. She finally got home and turned on the news. When she heard of the accident, she broke into tears because she knew she may have been in the accident or witnessed the accident if she took her normal way home.

She prayed that one day she would come in contact with someone that was impacted by the accident, and we both knew that it was not a coincidence that we were both on this trip meeting each other for the first time.

Since we had to clean our dishes and work as a team, I was paired up with a sweet, motivated, and warmhearted girl. We were laughing and having fun cleaning the dishes. Then the next day at the center, we actually cooked with each other. I knew Macy had something to do with the fact that I was in a kitchen because we all know how that goes.

At the end of the week, all the volunteers put on a book fair for the children. I was working with one of the girls who I became close with. The table we set up was for the teens of the center, and I was getting another outside-of-my-body feeling.

"Hey, *The Fault in Our Stars*, have you read this book? I heard the movie is coming out soon," I asked my friend.

She looked at me, and once again, I knew something was coming.

"My boyfriend has cancer for the second time, and that book reminds me of him," she said.

Oh boy, I thought to myself. *Look at what you got yourself, into Jess.*

Per usual, I ended up getting her whole life story and connected to her on some level. She became my saving-the-world-one-day-at-a-time buddy.

All four of them provided either a lesson, a smile, or a moment that I felt light coming through. They were all put on my journey for a reason, and I can't thank them enough for moving me so deeply that words cannot describe.

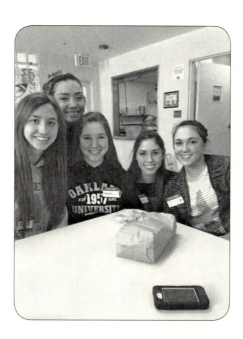

A couple of weeks later, my saving-the-world-one-day-at-a-time buddy's boyfriend died. I knew deep down what I had to face but did not make it a big deal to anyone. It was time for my soul to attend a funeral to learn I was not the only one in this world that was grieving.

I went to the mass with two of my friends from the trip. We sat up in the balcony with the aerial view of the church. I witnessed kids my age sobbing in the aisles and leaning on another. His teammates wore their team jacket in honor of him. His family sat in broken shock as the mass went on. I sat there in silence absorbing all the emotion. I sat there as if I was watching a part of my life, facing the truth and the adversity about the fact that even though I felt guilty, it was time to journey on from the pity party I was having for myself.

We stood up, and it was time for the bread and wine. Bowing my head as I walked to the altar, I made sure I would walk by our friend just so she knows we supported her, not to get praises like "Hey, we came for you" but to know she is loved and she is not alone.

I put my hand on her shoulder as she sat still. Once she saw who it was, her face looked like she saw an angel. Naturally, I turned around to see what she was looking at, but I realized what she saw was me. She stood up and collapsed on my body. The whole church was watching us as she wept. No words were spoken, no pictures were taken, and no questions were asked. The power of love took place. I just did not give the love and the support; I received the strength I have been praying for.

You know, it is funny. We ask for God to heal all and to create miracles, which he does. However, here is the catch, are you willing to face your fears in order to become the miracle and hope you strive for? I mean, I prayed and asked for healing, strength, and courage. The universe did exactly that but not in the way I would have liked. Think about how many times the universe has given you another chance but you were too stubborn or fearful of coming face-to-face with your wounds.

Challenging moments just don't happen in one day. They write a whole chapter of your journey. Some may just be pages, but some may be chapters. Events happen behind the scenes that make the fight so uniquely colorful. It is the silent cries in your car, it is the fake strong face that you put on to make people think you are fine, and it is the emptiness that fills your body although, in that moment, your mind gets foggy. Your eyelids don't want to blink because you are afraid of the realization that when you open your eyes, it is not just a scary dream. But when the universe offers you a second chance or a new beginning, take it. Open up your heart and just go for it.

Less than ten feet

I will never forget what he was wearing. He had dirty gray hair. His jeans looked like they haven't seen a washer in years, and his shirt was a white undershirt. He was alone sitting on the ledge of the wall, waiting for a court official to open up the doors to the courtroom. No handcuffs, no jail uniform, and no police around him. To strangers, he was probably just a guy who looked like he needed a shower. To me, he was the individual who killed my roommate and lifelong friend.

I was the first person to see him. I knew it was him as soon as I walked by him. Chills filled my body as I got closer.

What do you even say? What do you even feel when you are less than ten feet away from the individual who killed your friend?

To this day, he probably still doesn't know who I am.

Everyone sat together on one side of the courtroom, and he sat there as a ghost. No head motions or knuckle cracks. Just motionless.

Instant pain, suffering, and heartache took over the courtroom as soon as Macy's family walked in. This was just the beginning of a long journey of trials.

I sat there dumbfounded as I kept flashing back to when I had to stand up there in front of the judge. Ironically enough, it was the same courthouse, same judge, and same courtroom where my MIP trial took place.

I would be lying if I said I did not think about forgiving him. Half of me wanted to punch him, and the other half wanted to sit next to him and ask him about his life. *What about his family?* I thought. *Why is he alone? Did he drive here? Does he feel guilty?* Thoughts just consumed me as I debated in my head if I should forgive this guy or not. The trial lasted a very long time, but I will honestly say, in my heart, I forgave him. I never vocalized it to anyone or mentioned it to anyone, but here I am confessing it to you. But I didn't forgive him individually; I forgave life as a whole and made a promise to keep nothing but a loving space in my heart. I understood the lesson of forgiveness and how can I hold so much anger toward someone I really do not know. Yes, he was the driver behind the tragedy but he does not have the power to numb my heart. My heart needed love and peace. I forgave him so I could be free of allowing anger to guide my life. Was it hard to do? Of course, it was because I felt like I was failing Macy. Overtime my heart became alive again. I will tell you one thing I know for sure: Forgiveness is another key for soul growth.

Starting to believe

I was sitting at the receptionist desk at the audiologist office where I worked, just staring out the window. It was a gloomy day, and my mind was racing, just thinking about how I needed to find another internship and how life never stops. It secretly pissed me off because all I wanted was to wake up from this nightmare. Gloomy days make me think of all the negative crap and how I was still drowning. I never really admitted it, but I was drowning. I still was questioning everything; I was desperate to find meaning, like why does the color red mean stop and green mean go in an intersection. I am telling you. One day you are good and the next you aren't.

I was fearful of the future and what it would bring. I was too sensitive and raw, and the thought of getting turned away from an internship would most likely have pushed me overboard.

I had a whisper, and it was to apply for Special Olympics of Michigan. I am not even kidding—I reached out to a friend who had a contact with Special Olympics that moment and started to apply.

I also realized that I was so close to the deadline, so it was basically all or nothing at this point. I turned it in and just prayed for the best.

That afternoon, I got a phone call to set up an interview. Ecstatic is an understatement, but I did not let it get to my head because I did not want to get my hopes up. My interview was set up for Wednesday.

Hesitant and unsure of what to wear for my interview, I tried on about fifteen outfits before making a decision. Ironically enough, the office I would be working at was in Troy and right by my parents' new house.

As I walked into the supervisor's office, I got this pure, strong energy around me. It was in my soul, and it was growing. It was getting ready for whatever was going to come next. We walked down a hallway and ventured to his office.

The first thing I saw was the phrase "Why not?" written in red marker on his white board.

I froze. My knees almost gave out. Chills danced everywhere through my body.

The phrase "Why not?" is a phrase Macy is known for. She loved that phrase, and to see that phrase right in front of my face, I knew I was not alone in my journey, especially since it was Wednesday and the Share Her Spirit Movement created Why-Not Wednesdays. So that was my first sign.

The interview went surprisingly well, and it felt really refreshing to think about my qualities despite the dark times I was living.

Later that afternoon, I got a phone call from the supervisor—I got the internship.

Not going to lie, I got emotional after I hung up the phone with my supervisor. I guess I just was so grateful for the universe to actually show me it does have its good moments.

It was my first day of my internship, and I jumped out of bed and got ready with a bright smile on my face. I drove there without listening to music just so I could make sure I would take in the moment.

Two other interns were hired, and they got there before I did, which props for them. I sat down in the only open chair at the table and glanced at the floor. A penny heads up was right next to my chair.

"A penny!" I exclaimed out loud.

Cue the awkward stares from my fellow interns and my supervisors, but at the moment, I could care less.

To me, pennies are a gift from heaven. After Macy died, pennies and I became good friends. Once again, another sign that she was indeed helping me.

I picked up the penny with pride and put it right next to my notebook. A new chapter in my journey had just begun, and it was the start to the idea of belief.

After a couple of days, I could sense what intern I would work with best.

One was older and had her life together, very reserved but sweet. There was something about the other one though. She was adventurous and always talked. She was motivated and a hard worker. She was also honest, which I look for in people I allow into my life.

We got news that we had to attend an event, and we needed a certain type of shorts, which she did not have.

"Wanna go shopping together?" she asked.

"Well, sure! I'll go. I already have shorts, but I will go," I responded.

Little did we know that was the beginning of our friendship. We drove to the store and shopped for an hour or so. Hanging out with her was easy. She was laid-back and was actually interested in what I had to say. We talked about boys, food, clothes, school, etc.

The best part about the story is that when it was time to walk back to our cars, there was a downpour. We had no umbrellas or anything to cover us. We looked at each other and started to run. Laughing and giggling, we were dancing in the rain. It reminded me of the way I felt when I was with Macy—just on top of the world, loving every second spent together even if we were getting rained on.

We got to our cars, and everything was soaked. I had to sit on a random plastic bag I had in my car to make sure I did not stain my seat. Since that moment, we were known as the best friends interns of Special Olympics.

A couple of weeks later, we worked the Special Olympics summer games at Central Michigan University. We drove separate but followed each other the whole way there. I will never forget as we were driving on the highway, I saw her foot hanging out of the window. I could not help but burst out into laughter. I called her and asked her why her foot was out in the window, and she responded saying how she was bored and how her foot needed to breathe.

We roomed together and put on many events that weekend. We were a team, and I loved working with her. One night we got rebellious and went to the store and bought some champagne and drank the whole bottle. I opened up about my health and told her the story of Macy. She had tears in her eyes, and of course, a deep conversation happened. She also lost a friend in an accident and understood the heartache of adversity. We both knew it was not a coincidence that we met when we did.

Our summer was jam-packed with events for Special Olympics.

One day we were driving to a golf outing event, and we were talking about our friends who are in heaven.

"Oh my god! No way!" she exclaimed.

"What? What? What's wrong?" I asked.

"The GPS says we have to get off at Sheldon Road and turn onto Macy street," she said.

Silence and chills.

Sheldon was her friend that passed away.

"You are joking! There is no way," I said.

Sure enough, we exited onto Sheldon Road and turned onto Macy Street.

Now mind you, I realized that the internship was really not for me. I enjoyed it, but I realized I did not want to do that my entire life. I wanted more. But the lesson I did learn was this: what I needed most was a friend who was not part of my past. With her, I got a fresh start, a second chance, to allow new people into my life as well as accept who I am. Our friendship was key in my growth to start believing in the good again.

Your own grief

Everyone grieves differently. My own grieving journey guided me down a path filled with lessons about connections with other individuals.

The relationship I had with Macy's boyfriend was a connection I did not have with any one else during this process. At first things were great but then as we both dealt with our grief things spiraled out of control. Moments happened and words were spoken which can never be taken back. For a while we were not in constant communication like we were before. We have taken steps forward and I believe we both accept where we are in our grief process and being at different places is okay.

My relationship with her family is one of the most truthful relationships I have. It continues to teach me how important it is to be honest, respectful and open to communication. Our journey through this new normal continues to grow day by day.

My friendships were also tested by grief. At the time we all were just trying to figure out our lives let alone trying to live on with this horrific grief and without someone we love. A lesson that really touched me was the fact that there is no right or wrong during grief. This made acceptance really come in to play. Even if that meant a friendship that has been in my life for years stopped growing, that too is okay.

On the flip side some of my friends kept watering me while I was stuck in the dirt to help me grow and I will forever be grateful for that. Whether it was praying with me, going on walks, sending me a song or just a 'thinking of you' text, it moved me.

Center of it all

The hospital Macy went to was a hospital I have never been to before. Throughout those five days, it became our home; but after her death announcement, I couldn't even think of that place without cringing. I would purposely drive a different way to avoid the hospital if I had to pass it for some reason, which, of course, my journey guided me to—meaning, somehow, someway, I would one day have to face my fear of standing face-to-face with the hospital and relive those terrifying dark raw moments of my life.

It was wintertime 2014, and my mom asked me when I could come home because she needed to tell me something. Nervous of course, I drove home right away. She was crying and depressed. She was diagnosed with skin cancer. Now luckily, it was caught early, and we could control it. However, she needed surgery right away, and she needed someone to be there for her and take care of her. I told her I would reorganize my schedule, and we would make it work. A couple of days go by, and she scheduled her procedure, but once again, she told me to call her.

"Honey, I am so sorry . . .," she said quietly.

"Mom, what is it?" I said.

"I tried my best to schedule it someplace else, but I have to get it done where Macy went after the accident," she responded.

Instant chills and silent cries occur, and flashbacks start happening.

I could not believe it. I became fearful and worried about how I would react walking through the same halls again. It was as if the Divine knew I needed to release that fear and have it replaced with love and light.

On top of the skin cancer news was shared that she needed immediate attention to her female parts because test came back with possible cancer down there as well. I had enough and just broke down. I honestly thought I was losing my mom at the age of twenty-one. What mother has cancer in two different places and tumors on her brain? I became so angry with God and thought about giving up—unfortunately, this happened on many occasions. I was so afraid to experience loss again it ate me alive.

The relationship I have with my mother has been a rollercoaster of a journey. For months, we hardly spoke or even saw each other. I could not emotionally and mentally go home and witness someone who I love so deeply in pain, let alone be it my mother. I became defensive and very standoffish. Her depression was a very dark and hard one for my family.

When I would come home, I prayed for protection because I had no idea what I would walk into. Most of the time, there was no sunlight or positivity to be found anywhere. All the blinds were closed, and lights would be off, which was unusual for the Zacharias household. Growing up, we always had our front door and windows open, and music would be playing. It was no surprise to find my mom sobbing on the floor, screaming out in pain, or even popping pills like it was her job. I never understood why she took so many pills, and that did not go over well. Finding her puking in the bathroom or wearing her sunglasses on in the house became normal.

When my dad would go away for work, I would go home and stay with her because she was so unstable. The knives would be hidden, and my dad would push a couch against the back door so she couldn't escape. As we learned over time a lot of it was medicine induced. So we tried to start taking her of all of her medicine.

She will admit she has thought about taking her own life more than once, which, as a daughter, haunts me inside.

For a while, I felt as if her problems were more important than everyone else's. I mean, they are important, but it definitely affected my relationship with her because my solid ground just slipped from underneath me without my permission. I would say we were both depressed at the same time.

My mom and dad would always come to basketball games to come watch me dance, and for a while, my mom stopped coming because she couldn't get the motivation to or she was just too sick. For a while, I became jealous of people who had a close relationship with their mothers because a part of me lost mine. She lost her sense of humor, and she lost her love for this world. Emotional episodes would happen at least twice a week. I would have to stand there and take it and brush it off, but those words stuck with me.

A couple of days before her skin surgery, I went to the cemetery and had an emotional breakdown. I asked for a sign or confirmation that she would get through this time. As I was asking, I looked up and noticed a familiar car driving closer.

It was Macy's mom. Now this was the first time I have ever been at the cemetery the same time someone else was there. She parked her car and walked toward me. I noticed she didn't have a jacket on, which she always prepared for this type of weather, so I thought that was odd.

"Fancy seeing you here," she said.

I looked up and gave her a hug.

"Honey, are you okay?" she asked.

Cue the tears. I sobbed as she held me up. My mom and her are very good friends, and she had no idea that my mom was just diagnosed with cancer. She held me tight and told me she would be fine and she would make it through.

"I . . . I . . . I . . . have to go back . . . to the hospital where Macy died," I sobbed.

She looked me in the eyes and promised me everything was going to be okay and how she would be there for both my mom and me.

"You know, Jess, I was not planning on coming to the cemetery today. But as I was driving by, I had a very strong demanding push to come. Now I know why—to be here for you. Macy has brought us together," she cried.

From that moment, her mom and I have built a relationship that is so strong I consider her my second mother. Yes, we have our differences and our moments, but that is life. The fact that we could forgive one another and accept one another is proof on how powerful love can be. I am so blessed to have her and Macy's family in my journey.

After leaving the cemetery, something inside me changed. I went home and remembered giving my mom a hug. I started accepting the role I was assigned.

A couple of days go by, and it was time to drive my mom to the hospital. Now I would be lying if I said I didn't get choked up pulling into the same valet parking I did for those five days back in 2013. The same sliding doors opened, and this time, instead of running to see my friend on her deathbed, I was holding up my mom, guiding her to the waiting room. Flashbacks happened, but I fought to keep it together.

My mom was getting ready for surgery, and I gave her Lucky. She smiled and gave me her bracelet she would always wear when I would have surgery, especially when I was younger. I kissed her on the forehead, and she was off to surgery.

I walked alone to the waiting area and sat there by myself. I looked out the window and realized the view has not changed since I saw it last. Tears just streamed down my face, but it was almost as if those tears were emotions I needed to release. I then felt a sense of growth and strength. I honored my spiritual guides and my angels for guiding me to this place. As I ventured the halls, I heard, "Macy went to heaven from here. She started her new life here."

I then saw this hospital full of love and light. I thought about how many doctors and nurses helped Macy those five days. I thought about how this place is where the Divine guided her to her next journey with them. It was not her ending point, it was just the beginning. I guess I forgave myself too during this moment of growth. Because I understood my human instinct was to focus on the negativity and hate this place. But hate is just an illusion. It is not from the Divine or God, it is from the devil, and why would I let him control my heart?

My mom's surgery went well, and by this time, my grandma came to show her support. Even though it went well, my mom did keep getting sick. Nurses were concerned, but we kept telling them it was normal because it was normal to hold my mom's puke bag and not flinch.

I wiped her face, had ChapStick ready for her (knowing how easily your lips get chapped after surgery), and had cold towels ready for her to place on her head because her hot flashes were brutal. Yes, we giggled, but that was really when I fully accepted my relationship with my mother at that time.

We got her standing and dressed, and I became a pro at driving at the same time as holding the puking bag for my mom. My grandma followed us and got us some food—told you she loves to get us food.

A couple of days go by and my mom had her female procedure done. My dad was home for this one, and it was nice not having to wait in the waiting room alone. We took a walk and got coffee. Even though my relationship with my mother was rocky, it did give my dad and I time to enjoy each other's company. Now mind you, they both still annoy me sometimes, but that is what parents are supposed to do.

So what did I learn during this time? I learned that in order to grow, you must remove all the hate and negativity from your heart even if that means for you to stand in the center of the place that traumatized your view of this world. We all have a group of divine spirits working for us. When we allow them to guide us and teach us lessons, boy, is the growth magnificent. Now whenever I drive by the hospital, it is the hospital that started Macy's new journey and opened the new positive chapter of my relationship with my mom. I will be forever grateful for that hospital and for my journey for taking me there.

Always wear your crown

Experiences and moments grow an individual's heart, mind, body, and soul. As we live each day, hidden gems are among us. You can find them in a song, an encounter with a stranger, or even a fortune cookie. The list is endless. Challenge your eyes and view them as blessings.

As humans, we tend to forget about an aspect of life when we do not really have anything to complain about. Except in the time of need, it overwhelms you with a powerful force that takes you down a list of emotions you may not have been aware of their existence. My friends, what I am talking about is called *time*.

Time serves an illusion. One moment we love it, the next we wish it did not exist. It takes us to moments where we want more time with a loved one or urge for less time as we anxiously wait for news we pray is the answer to our prayers.

Time and I have a love-hate relationship. However, I am eternally grateful for the time I have received on this earth. Throughout my rollercoaster of a journey, my friend, *time*, guided me to the powerful, strong, and courageous lesson of what it truly means to wear your invisible crown and the back story of the sassy phrase.

Maintaining the positivity, hope, and faith became more of a tedious job rather than a lifestyle I strived for—heck, positivity is my middle name according to the outside world. I was seeking light in my darkness, while others looked to me as their light. Honored to be their light? Of course, but stress and pressure filled my heart, which would take years to overcome.

Here is the truth, challenging times just do not happen in one day. Wish it could be that way, but life is not the fairytale we want it to be. We all are struggling. Fighting for that moment of freeness. To have our bodies fill up with strength and dignity rather than darkness. However, that is what heaven is for. This life is for your soul to grow, to learn, and most importantly, to love. Your wounds will turn into scars. But that is not the point. The point is that your scars will turn into stories you can share with others. They are your tattoos that make you who you are. Give them time and love because once you do, time will provide you a sense of freedom that will be in reaching distance.

I did not just learn the importance of this lesson in one day. It was a journey in itself, let me tell you.

A lesson I was taught, which I thought was "normal," was typically when an individual puts in enough time and effort, they get the applause, especially when they are involved in a group or sport. Senior year is the year when you stand on top. Celebrations are about you and your accomplishments, the speeches are about how fantastic you are, and the seniors determine the ways of communication throughout the entire year. It is the year society has created to be the year to look forward to.

I will do you a favor and save you the sob story. Basically, I only made it to the pregame before the big party for my senior year on dance team at Oakland University.

What does that mean? It means I tore my meniscus in my right knee weeks before the first basketball game. Remember the knee I bumped before I saw the yellow light on the cruise ship? Yeah, same exact knee. Coincidence? I think not.

"An injury would not stop me" was my mind-set. As captain, how could I let the team down? To just give up? That is not how I wanted to be remembered as a leader. We added about fifteen freshmen that year. They needed someone who they could look up to, someone who could bring out the leader that lay inside of them.

Observing every practice and game as the cold ice would melt on my knee got easier and easier. The agony of not dancing got smaller, which I never thought would happen. I began to stand with a sense of honor and dignity for the team that I got to help build, but most importantly, lead as well.

On Tuesday, January 20, 2015, I woke up with no idea on where my journey would take me. Since it was Tuesday, I knew the structure of my day: counselor, work, OC for lunch, class, dance team practice—typical schedule I have had for the past four years, so nothing too special, or at least I thought.

God had a different plan for me that Tuesday.

It started off with me babbling about how happy I was to my counselor at nine in the morning. I kept going on and on about how much fun I had over the weekend with some of my teammates. I kept saying, "We were acting like sisters. No matter what we were doing, we just kept laughing, and it was so much fun." For me, I was on a whole new level of happiness. My counselor was somewhat surprised on how joyful I was with regard to my happiness since we have been working on it for a very long time.

I walked out of the health center with a smile on my face because memories just kept replaying in my head about the weekend. Then my phone went off. It was Macy's sister, and she said, "I didn't know Macy had a Tumblr. Look at the verse she has in her Tumblr profile."

The verse read, "For I know the plans I have for you. Plans to prosper to you and not harm you, plans to give you hope and a future," Jeremiah 29:11.

Thoughts ran through my mind about how comforting the verse was, so it stuck with me throughout my day.

Two of my teammates and I ate lunch together. These two call me Mother since I drive them everywhere, so I personally feel like we have a tight bond. We were giggling about the weekend, and in my head, I thought to myself, *Wow, I couldn't imagine my life without them. God is good.*

Class was normal, and then I went to meet with an individual who knows how to push my buttons. We lived together and also were teammates. I care for her very much, but I think if you asked her, we were not on the same page. Our friendship journey is a colorful one. Nerves filled my body, but I asked the angels to protect me and to share love and light even though my ego was not a fan of this idea.

Starbucks was our location for the next two hours, discussing topics that needed to be released off our chests and then allowing ourselves to move forward together. Forgiveness took place as well as letting go.

A compromise was made with regard to leading the team. She asked for the captain role because she claimed she was doing all the work, and I accepted without any hesitation, which, I'm not going to lie, I think I surprised both her and myself. My mind was saying, "What am I doing?" but then my heart told me, "It is time."

An expectation list was created by both of us with hopes and actions on how to end the season with a bang. This was a giant step for me individually even though we were moving forward as one—to start allowing my legacy on the dance team come to an end.

Our meeting was completed with both of us smiling and laughing. Passed along the info to the coach, and she was on the same page. Always believed everything happens for a reason and believed this season was something special.

As I ventured through the hallways of the O'rena on my way to practice that night, I walked onto the court and I felt at peace. My eyes noticed the littlest things, like spots on the wall, the obnoxious noise the doors make when you open them, or the new Travis Bader banner by the big screen. Plus, it was bright and had a special shine to it.

My body took a rest as I sat down and watched dance team practice. Around 8:30 p.m., it hit me. The realization and the overwhelming emotions of what meant the end to my dance career.

It was the realization that my purpose on this team was to guide it, to build it, and to leave a legacy, which I hope I did. I wobbled my way to the bathroom because I needed to be alone to understand my thoughts and emotions. My hands weighed heavy on the sink, and I slowly looked up in the mirror. I saw myself as a grown leader who achieved her assignment. I stared into my own eyes and accepted the role of the final stage of being a true leader.

My car is my safe haven, and I cried the whole way home after discussing my realization with two of my friends who spoke words of wisdom. Shouts and cries out to God took place to give me guidance on how to take the next step or to even provide me a sign that I am not crazy to think it was time to let go of dance team.

I entered my apartment with black mascara all over my face and ran to the bathroom. I paced back and forth, just unsure what step to take.

A little whisper came to me, and it said to open up my "Jesus Calling" book and turned it to the date January 20.

You know that sign I cried for on my way home? Well, God and my guardian angels gave it to me.

My eyes read the verse for the day, which ended up knocking me right to the floor.

The verse for January 20 read, "For I know the plans I have for you. Plans to prosper you and not to harm you. Plans to give you hope and a future," Jeremiah 29:11.

To remind you, this is the verse that Macy had in her Tumblr profile, which was sent to me that morning.

Crazy, right? Chills. Absolute chills.

I spent that entire night writing about the idea of serving and letting go. I wrote down every detail I could remember and accepted what had to be done. The next morning I met with my two friends who I spoke to the night before and discussed how I felt the morning after. I had them read my story, and they both agreed it was time. After thanking them for their support, I received a phone call from my mother.

Typical Jessica moment, I made this decision to let go of dance team without their consent because they were out of town in Virginia to see a new brain doctor. My mom was still not fully recovered from her first brain surgery. I answered the phone with fear because I was afraid of seeing my mother go through brain surgery again and to tell her I was done with dance team. She was crying on the phone and explained that she needed another brain surgery. Devastated and upset, I hung up the phone and knew my decision was made. I put the phone down and put my head into my hands.

After a couple of moments, I looked at my friends and said, "Everything will be fine. My mom has to have another brain surgery. Thank you for your help, and I will call you in a little bit." We then exchanged hugs, and they told me they would pray for strength to get through the day.

The next couple of days, I was emotionally sensitive. I was not just letting go of dance team, I, at the moment, was giving up dance as a whole. That thought left an unsettling feeling in my stomach, but I knew it was just the beginning. I wanted to share the news with my friends that my mom was having another surgery, but at this point, I was so afraid to tell anyone anything that I just kept quiet until someone asked if I was okay. It is funny because when things continuously happen to you, you know how to word the message to everyone you tell. Some just ask because they are curious, some just want to talk about it, some just want to use the knowledge to be able to say they "know" me that well, and some just are afraid of the thought that something like that could happen in this world.

I made a promise with myself that I would tell my coach as well as some special souls on the team about my decision. I took the captain and teammate hat off and put on my friend hat. I prayed that somehow, someway, I would get the chance to tell them all individually and not rush the moment. Surely enough, the next day I ran into all three of them on campus individually and sat down with each of them. The angels were with me because I have never seen all three of them on campus like that before. As I imagined, they cried and were shocked. They, however, understood and respected my decision, which shows what types of people they are.

Two days later, I announced I was letting go to give them the chance to grow as leaders and to make their mark on dance team just as I did.

Instead of hearing a speech about how amazing I was as a leader and dancer, I got the chance to wear my invisible crown, have the Lord applaud my decisions, and to provide a speech filled with love for people I adore. Allow time to guide you to moments where you can provide recognition for yourself and serve.

This stuff scares people. It even scares me. Everything I was blessed with was taken away from me, and all that was left standing in that moment was my purpose. Moments turn into lessons, lessons turn into truth, and truth turns into growth.

Your journey is not complete if some days are enjoyable and some days you just don't know what way to turn. Throughout my journey, I have urged for meaning, reasons on why certain situations happened and what was the point behind them. Struggling each and every day with physical, mental, and emotional pain on top of the unnecessary drama, "Honestly, what is the point?" I would scream in the car, praying for an answer, a direction. There was a stage in my life where I fought against everything. Looking back at it, that time, I was nothing but selfish. I thought I didn't deserve what was happening to me and what I had to go through. I thought I deserved better. It was me against the world. I did not hate my life by any means, but anger was present in my heart and soul.

I felt as if I had to prove myself to the people and to my world to show that nothing will knock me down. That notion did more harm than good. Once again, I became my own worst enemy. I did not really give myself time to heal until a year and a half later after the accident.

It was the same night where I realized what had to be done about dance team and to walk away from it. I stood there alone in my room, looking at all my pictures on my wall that took me a whole day to put together. It was three in the morning, and I knew there was no way I would get sleep that night. I stood there taking it all in but knowing that chapter was over.

"It is time. It is time to put on your real smile," I heard.

I ripped every picture off my wall, not because those friendships I had were done with but time had changed and I needed to look inward to become my own best friend because I had no idea who I really was. By doing that, I presented myself a fresh start. That's the thing, life always presents you a fresh start, but we, at the end of the day, have the choice to when that fresh start will begin. Free will, everybody.

Ripping those pictures off my wall was bittersweet, but I felt myself growing. My soul took its first breath.

Did I throw away the pictures? No. I put them in my picture box. But there I stood, nothing but white walls.

I gave myself the chance to really grow.

Yes, it was an ending to a chapter, but boy, the next chapter was filled with nothing but growth, love, and acceptance.

The lesson that I will share is this: When you allow your journey, the angels/your higher power/ the universe to guide you, your eyes will shift and your heart will shine. Soul acceptance will take place and that my friends is the definition of wearing your invisible crown.

The message from the mess

The journey of letting go of the dance team was a powerful one. It opened up a door that I was nervous but eager to open. My parents were being parents and were confused as to why I quit. I told them it was time, and I was letting go to give the girls on the team a chance to shine and to lead. One of the many phrases my dad still says to this day is plan your work, work your plan. Quitting was never in the plan so that went over well.

Because I did not hold the responsibility to lead the team anymore, it gave me the chance to guide and to lead my life. It was the beginning of a new year that held a lot of power. It was the year that I will graduate college—a day that my doctors never envisioned to happen. This gave me time to take a step back and think about what I wanted to become, accept everything that has happened and make something of it. I found myself writing a lot. I would write random simple statements that would come into my head or even at night, write about my day and the lesson I was grateful to learn. Writing, at the time, was my healer and another way of expression.

The last moment I shared with Macy was listening to the song called "I Lived" by One Republic in our bedroom, such a profound moment that will always be stored in my heart. Movement is what keeps me grounded, and boy, did I need it. After many thoughts and talks to myself, I finally had the confidence to ask my boss at the studio to allow me to do a dance in honor of Macy. Why? To allow the soul promise we made come to life and to celebrate her journey in a moving way.

Growing up at Gotta Dance, I always had this dream that one day I would be able to share my passion with the people I adored the most, the ones who pushed me and looked up to me: my little sisters. I wanted to provide them an opportunity to dance from the heart. In a divine way, my dream about creating a dance for my little sisters came true by sharing with them the story of Macy and me and our friendship.

The first day of class, we sat down and I told them the story. Their eyes filled with excitement but more of an understanding on how important it was. I had them close their eyes and listen to the song. Once the song was over, I made sure they knew it was not supposed to be a depressing dance but a happy one. Choreographing it, I knew it was going to be good, but I had no idea what was in store.

After months of practicing and rehearsing, it was time where I emotionally had to move forward to take that step and, rather than live it, to let it go and place the story into individual hands that will protect it. Learning how essential the dance was for my own personal growth was an escape for me to release emotions but also a way for my eyes to open the positive pure joy that was behind it all.

Competition time is when the expectations are raised through the roof and the rollercoaster of emotions start riding the tracks. My goal was for the dancers to be at peace but also to tell the story. The balloons were blown up, their costumes were on, the sunflowers were secured, and it was time. We gathered in a circle and bowed our heads. Once we hugged, I checked them in.

Alone, I ran.

Running to the stairs to sit up in the balcony by myself, I feared rejection. *Is it going to be good enough?* I thought. What if a balloon pops? What if the flower breaks? I closed my eyes and took some deep breaths.

"Please welcome to the stage, 'I Lived' from Gotta Dance."

The auditorium rumbled as the two dancers who played Macy and Jess entered the stage. They got into position and were ready to go. Music danced its way out of the speakers as the dancers captured the audience.

As the two were dancing, the rest of the dancers enter the stage with a balloon in their hand. At this point, there was no turning back. I sat as I watched them bring the piece to life, knowing that they could do it but not having a lot of faith in myself. Then something breathtaking happened. When the chorus began, some people in the audience stood up and started clapping and dancing. Then before you know it, the whole audience is clapping and even singing the song—not just dancers and families from our studio but the whole audience. The stage kept getting brighter and brighter. I then just let it out. My head fell into my hands as I wept, not upsetting tears but tears that meant that it happened. The vision came true, and it provided my soul meaning behind the tragedy. As the dance came to an end, I stood up and once again ran, ran to find the dancers. But it was not an easy path.

Everyone from the studio that knows my story grabbed me and hugged me. Some of my teachers who I have known for years and hardly ever cry were sobbing.

"These aren't sad tears. These are emotional, happy tears," everyone kept saying. "That was one of the most beautiful dances I have ever seen," said another.

It took me a while to understand how it was even possible to have happy tears while watching a dance that is in honor of someone who is no longer with us. But then I got it.

The dance provided light to those who needed it, to be able to celebrate their loved ones who have passed.

Sharing the news with her family that I choreographed a dance in honor of Macy was bittersweet, to say the least. The second competition was held at the high school we went to, which, I would like to point out, I have been with Gotta Dance for years, and we have never had a competition at this location. I was completely moved because I knew someone else was in control.

Unlike the first time the girls performed the dance, my mom, my grandma, and Macy's mom came and watched. She even brought me flowers! How adorable.

Nervous? Uh yeah. But the girls were ready. I introduced the dancers to Macy's mom as well as the dancers' mothers. Everyone was ready, and it was showtime. I sat next to my boss, and this was the first time she saw it in costume. After it was done, I looked at her, and she was crying. My boss never cries. I was so proud of the dancers and was eager to see what her mom thought about it.

The sky was blue, the air was warm, and the sun was shining. So I thought why not venture outside and release the balloons and take cute pictures to post on Instagram.

As we were getting ready, Macy's mom met us outside. She could not control herself. She was crying, shaking, and smiling all at the same time. With her arms wrapped around me, she kept saying, "Thank you. Thank you. Thank you." She wept on my shoulder for a couple of moments, and I knew that my promise to Macy about being there for the family was indeed coming to life.

The beautiful part about all of it was that every dancer had their parents outside witnessing it all. All these families I have known for years. I would have not wanted to celebrate Macy's spirit with anyone else that day.

She then hugged all the dancers, and everyone was crying. Pictures were taken, and memories were made. Yeah, we may not have won at the competition, but we got the chance to help heal a grieving mother's heart as well as sharing an angel's spirit.

Graduation day

It was the day that all undergrads spend four years of their lives for—graduation day, to walk across that stage to get a piece of paper. But the hilarious part of it all was that in that exact moment, your diploma wasn't even in the black fancy cover they give you.

The day was more than just that piece of paper though. For some, it was the beginning of their next educational studies; for others, it was that slap-across-the-face-holy-shit moment that they need to get their life together; and for some, it was a day that they expected to experience.

For me, it was the day I dreamed of when I would fight for my life while I lay in a hospital bed. Lucky for me, the Divine made sure that I would get to experience graduation day with some of my dearest friends who made an impact on my journey at Oakland.

You know my dance team friend, the one who sat with me in the emergency room and let me crash at her place during the time of the accident? Yeah, her. We met at her apartment, got ready, and ventured to the O'rena one last time. Once we got there, we realized we were cutting it close. The ceremony started at five, and we did not get there until four fifty-ish. But we didn't care. That was nothing out of the ordinary for us. After that, we separated and went to our specific lines.

I then got to spend the next couple of hours with my college day one. Literally, I met her my first day of college, and I knew it was not coincidence that we crossed paths.

She sat in front of me. She looked like she had her life together. Every day she would put her water bottle in the corner of her desk, pull her hair back, and slip an Altoid before class began.

Interested in her routine, but I had a feeling there was a reason why she did all those things. One day I had my hair up and she noticed my tattoo behind my ear, which says, "Journey on."

Not to make it a big deal, I just skimmed the conversation lightly and told her she would learn about it when I would give my first speech.

Oddly enough, she beamed with excitement and counted down the days until my speech. The day came where I pretended like I had my shit together and gave my speech. We had to pick three objects that described who we are. Think I did my family, dance shoes, and my tattoo.

Obviously, with my tattoo, I explained my health and where the whole idea of "Journey on" came from. I looked over at my friend, and she had tears in her eyes as if she saw an angel or something. I wanted to stop and ask her if she was okay, but I kept going on with my speech.

Once I was done, I sat down and asked if she was okay. She said, "Now wait until you hear my speech."

A couple of days went by, and it was finally her turn to present. That was the first time I noticed her walk. She limbed, and I thought maybe she had a hard day at workouts because she was on the swim team.

Boy, was I wrong. Similar to her, I teared up during her speech, also had chills the entire time. Long story short, she is a cancer survivor and was in remission. For the first time in my life, I came across someone who actually gets it—gets the way I view this world and gets what it means to fight for your life. Since that day, our friendship grew stronger and stronger. Ironically enough, she became captain of the swim team her junior and senior year. But the funny part about it is that no one knew how close we were. We would meet every other month and update each other and get leadership advice as well. She really was my college day one.

Fast-forward to graduation day and we never left each other's side. Talk about divine alignment and a God wink for both of us. We stood in line waiting to walk into the O'rena, and one of my high school classmates stood with us. I noticed he had a teal ribbon on his gown. I asked what it was for, and he said, "It's for Macy." Talk about emotional rollercoaster. So there I was, sitting in the O'rena in between the guy who was wearing a ribbon in honor of Macy and my college day one. I was experiencing my dream on so many unimaginable levels.

To be honest, after walking across the stage, I did not feel any different from before I walked across the stage. It is just the way we as a society run the idea of graduating.

We then got the applause from family and friends and the ceremony was finished.

Now long story short, things went downhill from there. My parents and I had a huge miscommunication. This is what was going on in my brain. After graduation, stop at my friends house, go home and have dinner with my family. Well, that did not work out.

There I was standing alone, taking pictures of my friends and their families at graduation. Now mind you, we took pictures before, but still, I was sensitive and my emotions were high, and I was at a high risk of getting triggered. My dad called me to tell me they were going to dinner with my cousin who also graduated. Upset and confused, I asked if I could meet up with them since I did not want to be alone celebrating my graduation.

We met, and everything hit the fan. Now when one of your parents is sick, you learn to choose your words very wisely and do your absolute best to not offend them because it is not their fault. Especially in my mom's case, it was her tumor talking. Most of the time, I kept thoughts to myself and just let it go because it was not worth the fight. But this time, I fought for myself. It was my graduation, and they were going to dinner with my cousin. Love them dearly, but I was being selfish and I was pissed.

I drove to my friend's house with thoughts of confusion and frustration. I did not want to let it ruin my day, and I tried so hard to not take it personally. Going to my friend's house just made it that much harder.

I walked in and saw nothing but love, balloons, cake, pictures, presents, food, laughs. You name it—it was a party. Everyone was celebrating her accomplishment, and I was beyond jealous and bitter. I gave her a present, chatted with some friends, and ran out of there as fast as I could, not because I did not want to be there for her but because I just could not be there.

As soon as I opened up my car door, the well-known sobbing tears streamed down my face. I honestly do not even know why I was crying. I think I was just overwhelmed with everything.

On my way home, I pulled over, turned my car off, sat there, and just cried. I needed that time to sob and realized what the hell was going on. Change—that was what it was. Change was happening in more ways than one. I knew I was loved, I knew I did it all, I knew people were proud, I knew I accomplished my dreams, and I knew everything was going to be okay. But I just felt like something was missing.

I then screamed to God, swearing at him and telling him how angry I was. "Why did you change my mom? Why am I alone on my graduation day? Why are you doing this to me?" Once I was done crying, I got myself together.

I drove home, and my dad was waiting in the driveway. He apologized for what happened and said that my mom was not feeling well. They did not mean to hurt me or make me sad, but my mom was reacting to her radiation.

I prayed for protection and guidance as my mother, father, and I sat in silence eating lobster and crab. Once we were done, I said good night and went to bed.

The next morning I jumped out of bed as if I was late to work. I didn't set an alarm, and I was confused as to why I literally flew out of bed. I stood there in silence, looked at the clock, and was unaware on what was going on. I then heard the whisper, "Go to church."

I did not want to argue with whatever I was hearing. To be honest, I thought I was still dreaming. So I got ready, and halfway through my morning routine, I stopped, looked in the mirror, and asked myself, "Am I really going to church?"

My mom, surprisingly enough, also was planning on going. We drove separately because we are the same person and needed our space since we weren't healed yet from the night before. The church is right by our house, and I have always had this feeling to go and experience it, but I never went for it.

We walked inside, and a gush of loving energy filled my heart. I got emotional for no reason. My mom and I picked a spot, and the mass began. What was the theme? "Singing in the Rain." How did God communicate to me? By having the kids of the church dance, sing, and perform throughout the entire mass. A video was then played featuring little kids talking about tough times and how they got angry with God. One little girl, who had brown hair, talked about how her sister was in a car accident.

I sat there sobbing. But not like the night before. Sobbing tears of joy and growth.

I then noticed a taller blond-haired girl getting ready to perform by herself. This girl looked familiar to me, but I was not sure why. Her hair was in a bun, and it looked like she was a dedicated, well-put-together dancer. All the kids exited the stage, and she entered with her back facing the audience. The way she moved was as if I have watched her dance before. The song was about dancing through hard times, and the way the stage was set up, she was dancing on water, and water poured down from the ceiling. It was magnificent, and I knew my prayers and screams the night before were listened to.

She then turned around, and I could not believe my eyes. On that stage was Amber, my roommate. I completely lost it. My mom handed me tissues, and I could not control myself and said, "Oh, I forgot to tell you—this is where Macy went to church." Queue the tears I did not even know I had in me.

Yes, Amber and I have our past, and there was a time when we both didn't see eye to eye, but seeing her on that stage was my sign that Macy wanted us to be friends again. I contacted her after mass and asked if it was her dancing. Indeed, it was. And guess what, we entered a new chapter of our friendship, and it was what I needed to believe in life again. Learning that the universe is for us and not against us is a lesson that actually does change your life.

From that day, I expanded my idea of spirituality. I was blindsided by the love that my angels and God provided me. Since that day, I have put all my true faith into them and know that they are with me every step of the way.

I lived

It was summertime, and I received a message from Macy's mom asking if the dancers would like to perform the dance at the golf outing benefit, which is put on for the Share Her Spirit Movement. I was stunned, absolutely honored but stunned. To be honest, as I watched it the last time at recital, I felt a sense of energy that was saying that it was not the last time they would be performing it. I thought I was weird and strange and that was my ego talking to me, so I just pushed the thought away. But then here I am, reading a text from her mom asking if the dancers could perform it. Of course, we went for it.

Time passed and it was the week of the golf outing. It was time for me to relive the night before the accident and talk about the conversation we had in front of everyone at the golf outing. It was my time to grow.

I was anxious. Fear again was present. Thoughts like "What if I mess up?" or "What if the podium is to tall?" flowed through my mind. I knew what I wanted to say, but I wasn't sure on how. I asked the angels for help, and surely enough, they did. Yes, I was stubborn and kept trying to change what they were having me say, but I just let it be.

News was brought to me that a dancer would not be able to perform at the golf outing because of another commitment. So I ended up speaking and then dancing. My invisible scars were becoming visible but in a loving and healing way. All my wounds were being healed but opening them up to share them with others. The speech was tough to do, but I knew it had to be done. Her family stood behind me while the dancers stood next to me. My soul knew angels were present. I could feel them calm my throat down and guiding me to speak clearly and effectively. The message moved everyone. I saw my mother crying, my brother putting his head down, and heard the tears from everyone in the room.

Yes, it was emotionally and physically challenging, but my soul stood as the messenger, and I will be forever grateful. After the speech was done, I ran. The thought of being the center of attention freaked me out, so running to the green grass area where we were going to perform the dance was my destination.

My heart and mind were calm. My soul felt free. It was at that moment where I learned the importance of my role on this world, which is a wounded healer. The phrase "Everything that is happening to you is happening for you" came to life. The music started, and there I was dancing with my little sisters on the grass with the sun shining and the wind blowing, celebrating Macy and accepting my role. Plus, it was the first time since I actually performed in front of my family and friends since my knee surgery.

The dance brought so much love and light to everyone at the outing. Amber, Macy's sister, and I had a why-not moment and went to Canada that night! To be able to laugh with them again and make more memories, I knew the circle had made its way around. I began to realize that the Divine was really on my side. I was starting to allow my journey to shine again.

Just two days later, I gave a speech about post traumatic stress disorder in front of my summer psychology class since I was taking the class to get ready for my master's. Here is a funny, typical Jessica story about this speech: You see, speaking in front of people does not bother me as much as some people. Yes, I am human and get the butterflies, but once I say that first word, the rest is smooth sailing. Well, at least now, I pray. The first couple of weeks of class, my professor announced how we will have many exams but also a final project and paper. The paper was obviously going to be about dance therapy, so that was a no-brainer, but the project had to be about another topic and it had to be with a partner. So as we picked partners, I was guided to say yes to this individual who I knew was going to be a challenge for me. She spoke whatever was on her mind, and some of the energy I got was not so great. My ego was screaming no, but my intuition told me to say yes. As I said yes, she interrupted me and told me how she already had the topic picked out. Secretly annoyed because the topic was something I was not really interested in, I just smiled and said okay. A couple of weeks went by and because of the universe and its crazy ways, she never showed up to class again. After reaching out to her in every way I could, I had to tell my professor that my partner was nowhere to be found. Of course, this was the day when he picked the order of presentations and guess whose presentation was picked to go first? Yep. You guessed right—mine.

Nervous and actually quite baffled, I told him that my partner probably dropped the course. He told me I had to do it by myself, which I took as an opportunity. I asked if I could switch it to a topic I was passionate about, and with ease and grace, I got to choose what I spoke about. The speech was twenty to thirty minutes. The day arrived, and it was my time to shine some light. Everyone was freaking out about their presentation and did not even realize I was all alone and had to go first. My heart was beating like a warrior, and my voice was getting ready to speak universal truth. The Divine was with me as I stood up there all "alone." At first, people were almost giving me that pity audience look when I first started because they felt bad for me, but then everyone was blown away and enlightened. It was such a gratifying feeling to watch other presentations, and they somehow related it back to mine. Now I wish I could be that cool and said I did it all by myself, but the true honor goes to my divine team for always coming up with the moments for me to grow. Once again, my soul served as the messenger, and I felt important. I was on a path of soul acceptance.

Wounded Healer that Shines

Y ou see, I am someone who changes my mind a lot and follows
her intuition every day, which it does, quite frankly, change day
to day. I was guided to attend workshops to enhance my intuitive
skills. Honestly, I thought I would just get information that I could
share with my students or even just some fun keep-in-the-pocket-type
information. You see, that is the funny thing. I always think I know
what is going on, but every time I think that, the universe continues
to show me I still have much to learn. Always have and always will. I
had no idea the importance and the essential growth of the path of
enlightenment and soul acceptance I was walking.

The first class I attended was called a shamanic journeying class.
If you asked me what shamanic journeying meant, I would have
looked like a deer in headlights, but I felt I needed to go. So after the
fear settled down, I listened and went for it. The chairs were set up
in a circle, the lights were dim, and angelic music was playing. In
some divine way, I felt at home even though I knew no one in the
class besides the teacher and I was also the youngest. I felt as if the
perspective of the uncertain world was completing its full circle and
showing me what this world is really about. What we learned and
practiced was leading with our soul and traveling to the upper and
lower worlds. Now what I learned is a nondenominational practice—
meaning, the practice enhances your spirituality and connects
you closer to the Divine. The Divine is God, who serves love and
light that serves the highest good for all. Yes, I still pray and go to
church; however, anyone can do this. Why? Because just like we
are all humans, we are also all souls, souls that are connected by
love and light. It does not matter what color of skin you are or what
language you speak, everyone has the power to lead with his or her
soul. However, in this middle world, it is not necessarily the "right"
thing to do. Basically, it is similar to a foreign language to lead with

your soul because this world is focused on leading with its ego and letting fear be its guide. You must go to school to get good grades, you must succeed in every activity you do, and you must get a good job so you can make enough money. That's the invisible formula that has been imprinted in our brains. My question is, and I have always asked this question, has that way of living really worked?

Okay, with all that being said, I respect it; however, there is so much more to this life than that. What I am about to share with you may be uncomfortable to the ego, but do your best to keep on moving forward.

The body we have is the house for our soul in this lifetime. With being human, two aspects we have are free will and ego—two aspects that influence our journey in this world. What I like to share with others is that ego stands for Edging God Out. Now whatever your view of God is, I respect it. I am not just saying that, I really do because my version of God has expanded overtime. To me, God is in all of us and is everywhere. All I urge is for you to believe in your soul and believe in the light that serves the highest good of all. Your soul has its own language. For example, soul language to me is joy, love, laughter, dance, happiness, etc. We all know how our bodies feel when we experience each one of those moments. A quote to ponder on is this: "We aren't human beings having a spiritual experience. We are spiritual beings having a human experience."

During this journeying class, we calmed the ego down through mediation, cleaned our chakras, and then got the opportunity to travel to the upper and lower world.

When someone dies, they travel to a different realm. Some believe you either go to heaven or hell because that is what they were taught when they were young. Not saying that is wrong or a negative thought, however, your soul goes through many lifetimes. In each lifetime, you have the chance to allow your soul to grow or lead with your ego. I personally do not believe in hell. I believe that there are many different realms we can go to. I have learned that once our physical body dies, our soul travels to a place where we are surrounded by angels. During this stage is when we watch our life review. We watch it and also feel it—meaning, the joy, the friendships, but also the grief, the sadness, and the hurt. But it does not last a long time. The point of the life review is to see how you lived. Did you live the best life you could? Did you follow your heart and soul? Did you allow the Divine in? Did you fulfill your soul's contract? Now depending on the growth of the soul, the next phase is up to the soul—staying in love and the light or lining up to come back down to earth. Told you this is mind blowing! How is your ego doing? If triggered, write down your thoughts and then come back to the book.

Now here is another aspect to ponder on. Some may have heard of it, but others may not. You sign a soul contract. Now, at first, I absolutely hated this idea. Why would I dare choose to live with all the physical and emotional pain I have experience? Why would I want to walk a path not many my age have walked? Why would I place certain people in my life that brought pain and suffering? Something to help me ease the thought was the idea that 80 percent of the situations in your life are divine alignment, and then 20 percent is this world's chaos. So I am not saying you chose every single thing in your life. You choose your purpose, your family, your friends, your lessons, and your growth. Now it all seems easy when we are in the light, and then when we travel down to earth, that is when we get our free will and ego. Some people let their soul fall asleep because their ego is so powerful. Some are in that tunnel of figuring out what their soul consists of and what to do next. Some are deep in religion because it allows them to feel connected to a higher power. But to me, the awesome thing about spirituality is that there is no religion. There is only love, light, joy, fulfillment, and soul growth. That is what we are meant to do—to grow, to love, to fulfill, and to accept our soul contract. It is just a matter of if we allow ourselves to do it. I would like to present a thought to you for you to ponder on: When our physical body dies, what does our spirit look like? Is it the color of our skin? Or is it the love and light that is within each and every one of us?

As I am learning about these different worlds and realms, my curiosity expands and my soul starts to be fulfilled in ways I never thought it would. See, there I go again, thinking I know shit. I became more confident in believing in the higher power, and instead of seeing this world in black and white, I began to see color—color in the leaves, color in a person's smile, and color in my family. Situations started showing up for me, and my journey was bringing light.

That summer, I was guided to attend another workshop that my teacher was putting together. It was Intuitive Empowerment. I knew I had to sign up, so I did it. But I want to make something clear.

Walking into a room where you are the youngest by twenty years is not easy, people. My ego was having a hissy fit, but my soul felt at home every single time I was learning and expanding my spirituality.

This empowerment class was a five-week series. We met once a week, and boy, that was a journey in itself. I learned how to clear chakras, got guidance from the Divine, learned about other people's journeys, and most importantly, gained confidence in myself.

You know how on the first day of school you pick a seat and for the rest of the year that is your seat and no one else's? Well, that happened in this workshop. I sat next to the same people every single time. I loved going and exploring. I was beginning to feel that peace I have been searching for.

During this time, I was also guided to explore Reiki-energy healing. I took a workshop and became Reiki-certified. I volunteered at Henry Ford Hospital where I worked in the greenhouse and served soul food to the patients.

I was then guided to take a trip of a lifetime. "Go to Sedona," I heard. "Just go for it."

My eyes bounced back and forth from the amount of the trip to my bank account. "I can't do it," I said to myself, and then I heard, "You are going!" By the grace of God, it happened.

This path I have been on is one that moves very quickly. I find myself asking my guides to just allow me to be still for a moment. Before I knew it, fall 2015 arrived. My mom and dad left for a couple of weeks to travel to Virginia for my mom's Cushing's disease, leaving me alone on the two-year anniversary of Macy's accident and when she went to heaven. As I hugged my parents one last time, a gush of energy filled my soul and told me, "It is going to be okay. This is the time to heal yourself. You aren't alone. Plus, your mom will be fine." Accepting the message, I dedicated those two weeks to taking care of myself. I was guided to walk nature trails I have never been on, learning and using essential oils, and most importantly, being still. I would sit outside facing the sun for hours on end—just being still, holding love and light to Macy's family and friends and to myself, using the tools to calm my fear down and knowing my mom will be okay. The thought of honoring myself at first was something I didn't quite understand. But if you take away anything from this book, I hope you begin your journey of self-care, really honoring who you are, to bring light to your magnificent soul, to understand where your fear comes from.

Yes, I cried here and there, but the amount of love I had for the uncertain world was universal. I have never allowed myself to witness so much beauty.

On October 23, Amber and I got breakfast together. You see, my plan was get breakfast and just chill at my house. Life had another plan. Amber and I ended up having our own bar crawl. We called it the why-not bar crawl. We went to four different places, and we had a blast. To be able to experience that with her and to know we both have in a way healed from the tragedy was just another circle that the universe guided us to complete. That girl will always have a special place in my heart and soul.

Before I knew it, I was at the mall with the purpose of getting yoga clothes for Sedona. As I was walking, I literally felt my guides stop me and guide me to another store. I shook my head as if I did not want to listen, but I went for it. I was guided to a corner in the store, and the sign said, "Sedona sweater." I laughed out loud and thought I was dreaming. So then I thought, *Okay, I would like a shirt that has feathers on it.* I heard, "Look up," and boom—what do I see? A beautiful shirt that had feathers on it. I couldn't believe it. That night I packed and suited up for a journey of a lifetime. I knew of my roommate because I met her in another workshop; however, she was more of a familiar face.

I ironically had to set my alarm at five o'clock in the morning. I woke up with butterflies in my stomach but excitement in my soul. My dad made me eggs and drove me to the airport. I have to say I loved it! We talked, laughed, and sang. We arrived at the airport, and he hugged and kissed me goodbye. Not going to lie, I got choked up. It was so precious. For the first time in my life, I was flying on a plane all by myself.

My Sedona roommate also had the same flight as me, which was crazy because mostly everyone else on the trip had different flights. We hugged and exchanged our emotions about the trip. It was then time to fly.

As we were boarding the plane, my smile was getting bigger and bigger. I picked the window seat because I love viewing the world from that view. The two other passengers in my row were already seated. There was a cute little old man sitting next to me. He was wearing a green shirt and had this huge smile on his face.

Since I was still in my little own world zone, I began to color. Art therapy, people, really works. Anyway, I could sense him observing me color. I then unplugged my headphones, and he smiled and said, "You know, you can color outside the lines."

I giggled and then started conversation.

His wife and daughter both passed away. He goes to Sedona every six months to visit his daughter's studio and stays there for a month and paints. He said he would paint with his daughter all the time, and he told me of how much his daughter loved Sedona. He told me to keep on going, to never give up, to go out and follow my dreams, but most importantly, to not be afraid to color outside of the lines. To the man in the green shirt from Winsor, I deeply thank you for sharing your light with me.

Our hotel was two hours away from the airport, so we had to rent a car. Instantly, my roommate and I had great energy. She was cracking me up. She is that person that has hilarious one-liners that you can't get out of your head and then switches to a deep heartfelt conversation.

I provided my life story, and she did the same. I took in the scene of Arizona. I have never been to this side of the country, so I was just amazed at the beauty.

As we checked in, I couldn't help but laugh out loud when I found out our room number.

No. 232.

"Do you have any ties to those numbers?" I asked.

"Yes, I do. Why?"

"Because I do too." I smiled.

We both knew that things were just getting started.

Our days would start with yoga, juicing, and then class all day long. You see, my plan was to attend yoga every day, but that only happened the first day. Why? Because my wonderful divine team would provide situations for me to use the lessons I learned in class at any given hour of the day and at night. My roommate too.

I have been guided to keep what I experienced sacred to me and whom I experienced it with. But I will say those souls are my tribe. The amount of soul healing I experienced was mandatory for me to continue forward. Plus, don't be surprised if I buy a house in Sedona.

I left behind my childhood suffering, self-doubt, and grief. I am taking with me soul acceptance, confidence, and healing.

So now what am I doing with my life? Funny you should ask!

My relationship with my family is deeper than it has ever been. I am so moved and grateful for their souls. Yes, I believe we would all say we are still working on some situations, but for the most part, the light at the end of the long tunnel has been shown to us.

My mom is getting better, but she is still sick. She is on her own journey, and I am so eager to see what happens for her. I ask that you keep sending her love and light whenever you can.

Me, on the other hand, I am serving my soul's purpose, which is to shine universal truth that moves individuals to love and light.

How? Another great question.

Dancing, moving, writing, creating, speaking, healing, and much more. The universe is shifting, my friends, and it is time to hop on board.

As this story is coming to a close, know that this is not the end. It is just the beginning, for all of us. I encourage you to look into your soul and really see what you are made up of. We all are souls made up of love and light. My friends, it is time to shine that light to fill this planet with love. We all are messengers of the Divine. We were made for one another to learn, laugh, and grow with one another no matter what color of skin you have or what language you speak.

Starting today, speak your soul language.

Once you start doing that, your journey will shine just as bright, and the entire world will be honored to experience it.

For me, I don't know where my journey will take me next, but I have faith it will be divine. I may go to grad school, write another book, speak around the world, start a nonprofit, or learn how to cook. But keep in mind, I currently am typing this downstairs in my parents' basement. Hey, a girl can dream!

I honestly have no clue. Don't be surprised if you ask me this society norm question "What are you doing?" or "Where are you working?" that my response will be simply this: "I am living."

Before I close, I just want to express my gratitude toward you. Thank you for allowing me to be vulnerable and share the real journey behind my shine. I am so honored to be able to share it with you in this way. But more importantly, I am eager to see your journey shine just as bright.

Last thing I will share is this:

An aspect that is certain in this *uncertain world* is that we were put here to grow. Our soul's growth comes from *learning to be comfortable with the uncomfortable.* We all will experience a *divine storm*, no matter if we like it or not. Altering your mind-set to *accept the unexpected* will take you to new levels of growth. We all, in some manner, have been wounded. It is up to you to become one that transforms into a *wounded healer that shines.*

What are you waiting for? go!

"Everything that is happening to you is happening for you."

Sending love and light to every single one of you, beautiful souls. Always shine and journey on my friends.

Jessica Zacharias

Acknowledgements

Throughout my journey I continuously have been blessed in more ways than imaginable. This quest of writing a book has been one of my biggest teachers from the universe up to date. However, the amount of loving souls I have been able to share it with is what truly makes my heart full.

To those of you who went walks with me, prayed with me, took me to your church and shined light on me, I thank you. To those of you at the studio who have been there since day one, I thank you. To my hilarious, crazy, fun, loving students, thank you for reminding me on how important it is to let your inner child shine. To those who hurt me, thank you. To my family who has accepted me for who I am, thank you. To my teachers and coaches, thank you. To my traveling buddies, thank you. To those who have shared their scars with me, thank you. To the creator of all things, the divine, angels and messengers, I bow down to you. Thank you for allowing me the opportunity to shine true light from this journey and allowing me to dance through it all.

Autobiography

Jessica Zacharias is a young female who has experienced adversity on various levels of life. She has survived over forty surgeries and has danced her way through her three-year life expectancy. With having a never-ending list of medical illnesses, she found her way of getting through it by expressing herself by movement. Dance brought foundation to her uncertainty. It brought her self-love, body awareness, and confidence.

Her life took a turn when her college roommate, who was also a very close childhood friend, was killed in a car accident. Living on from this tragedy has been one of the most heart-wrenching journeys she has been on. However, she found herself dancing through the pain, sorrow, and grief.

While she was grieving, her mother was diagnosed with a rare medical illness that produces pituitary tumors. This brought depression and mental illness right to her face as she proceeded to journey her way through.

Jessica is a wounded healer. Her soul purpose is to shine universal truth that moves individuals to spiritual awakening, love, and light. She serves as a dance teacher at the studio she danced at growing up. Her students range from the young children to young adults. She also helps out with the class for special needs students called My Time to Shine. Jessica is also involved in an outreach program that brings art to underprivileged children in a local community.

Being a communicator, Jessica knows that spreading the truth comes in many forms. You can find her writings and podcasts on her website: www.shiningjourney.com.

Jessica plans to bring love and light to her generation and to the younger generations. Being only twenty-two with all this life knowledge is being put to use as she shines her light.

People know her as the always-shine-and-journey-on girl.

Edwards Brothers Malloy
Thorofare, NJ USA
February 29, 2016